THE KONZA POETRY PROJECT PRESENTS:
Somewhere Between Kansas City and Denver

Edited by Jason Ryberg

Spartan Press
Kansas City Missouri

Spartan Press
Kansas City, MO
spartanpresskc@gmail.com

First Edition 1 3 5 7 9 10 8 6 4 2
ISBN: 978-1-950380-05-3
LCCN: 2019933165

Design, edits and layout: Jason Ryberg
Cover image, title page and exit images: Jon Lee Grafton

The Konza Prairie is owned by The Nature Conservancy and Kansas State University, and is operated as a field research station by the university's Division of Biology. It is one of 26 sites within the Long Term Ecological Research Network.

It has a continental climate characterized by warm, wet summers and dry, cold winters. Average annual precipitation (32.9 in, 835 mm) is sufficient to support woodland or savanna vegetation; consequently, drought, fire and grazing are important in maintaining this grassland. The site is topographically complex with an elevation range from 1050 to 1457 ft (320 to 444 m). In addition to the dominant tallgrass prairie, Konza contains forest, claypan, shrub and riparian communities. Limestone outcrops are found throughout the landscape.

Konza Prairie is located within the largest remaining area of unplowed tallgrass prairie in North America, the Flint Hills. Konza supports a diverse mix of species including 576 vascular plants, 31 mammals, 208 bird species, 34 types of reptiles and amphibians, 20 kinds of fish, and over 700 types of invertebrates. A herd of approximately 300 bison is maintained on the Konza, and native white-tailed deer and wild turkey are often present in large numbers.

Members of the public are allowed onto portions of the Konza Prairie through three loop hiking trails (approximately 2.6, 4.5, and 6 miles).

The Flint Hills, historically known as Bluestem Pastures or Blue Stem Hills, are a region in eastern Kansas and north-central Oklahoma named for the abundant residual flint eroded from the bedrock that lies near or at the surface. It consists of a band of hills stretching from Kansas to Oklahoma, extending from Marshall and Washington Counties in the north to Cowley County, Kansas and Kay and Osage Counties in Oklahoma in the south, to Geary and Shawnee Counties west to east. Oklahomans generally refer to the same geologic formation as the Osage Hills or "the Osage."

The Flint Hills Ecoregion is designated as a distinct region because it has the most dense coverage of intact tallgrass prairie in North America. Due to its rocky soil, the early settlers were unable to plow the area, resulting in the prevalence of cattle ranches as opposed to the crop land more typical of the Great Plains. These ranches rely on annual controlled burns conducted by ranchers every spring to renew the prairie grasses for cattle to graze. This has created in an unusual alliance between the native ecosystem of the Flint Hills and the people who use it.

The Heartland is an American political term referring to U.S. states that "don't touch an ocean," whether the Atlantic or Pacific, or to the Midwestern United States. The phrase not only refers to a tangible region but is also a cultural term connoting many ideas and values, such as hard work, rustic small town communities, rural heritage, simplicity, and honesty. Citizens of the Heartland—referred to as simply "Heartlanders"—are often seen as Blue collar.

There is no consensus as to "where" America's heartland is physically located. However, the American Midwest is the most commonly cited area as being the nation's heartland, although many other places have been referred to as part of it, often extending to rural or farming regions in the great plains. At least as early as 2010, the term Heartland has been used to refer to many so-called "red states", including those in the Bible belt.

The geographic center of the 48 contiguous U.S. states is near Lebanon, Kansas. When Alaska and Hawaii were admitted to the Union in 1959, the geographic center of the United States moved from Smith County, Kansas to Butte County, South Dakota.

Halford Mackinder, a British geographer, coined the word in 1904 to refer to the heart of the Eurasian land mass: a strategic center of industry, natural resources and power. The use of the term "heartland" to apply to the American Midwest did not become common until sometime in the 20th century.

TABLE OF CONTENTS

Somewhere Between Kansas City and Denver

Winter Ocean Rock by Glory Benacka

Gary Lechliter

I Shoot a Cardinal for Christmas

Because it's sitting on a dried stem,
and because no one stops me,
no angel in the woods to grab me by the throat,
or ghost of reason, or God herself.
Because I am fourteen and out of touch
with honor, I aim the air-rifle and fire.

The shot's so true the crimson bird
falls and throbs in the snow.
Still alive, it clacks its beak
and weakly sings for the moment.
Then, knowing what I have done,
I chill in the northern wind.

And brushing the snow, I make a small
burial site for the bird, cover it
gently and, with no idea what to say,
I fire a shot in the air for a one gun
salute, and trudge sadly home
through the beige fields.

Rubber Baby Buggy Bumpers

a tongue-twister revised

Someone should call the police!
For who could vet such a thing?
Rubber babies riding on buggy bumpers!
Or did I misinterpret the rhyme?
Baby buggies with rubber bumpers
are much more appealing and safe.

Or perhaps the buggy babies infested
with lice and those awful pinworms
are targets for rubber bumpers.
Which will surely cause angst
in the general population, or else
be classified as urban legend.

Rubber buggy baby bumpers?
It cannot be allowed in our country.
No one could get away with bumping
babies crawling in their diapers
in the path of rubber buggies
loosed by careless manufacturing.

And who can validate buggy rubbers
that terrify tykes in their blissful
sleep, those soon to be startled awake
by bellicose babies, eyes wild, drooling,
their prams about to sideswipe
the baby bumpers, stalled in traffic.

They Don't Make Days Like They Used To

They don't make days like they used to,
when each dawn was so unique
they called it blessed and threw away the mold.

Those were the days remembered.
While others we gladly forgot,
the ones wedged with Sunday School
that taught us to fear the night.

They don't make night like they used to,
when we sat in the timothy past bedtime
and gazed at constellations with awe.

They don't make wonder like they used to.
Now we see galaxies through telescopes
fixed on the glitter of distant stars
that waltz with celestial chaos.

J.T.Knoll

Just happy it starts

Rebecca, one of my mother's new caregivers, came up from Louisiana with her two kids to live with her mother six months ago. Drives a 2004 Crown Vic that shows the shadow of the Louisiana Highway Patrol emblem on the door. I noticed the driver's side window was down one cold December morning just before Christmas as I walked to the house. When I asked about it she said, in a slow Slidell drawl, that she was waitin' on her paycheck to buy a part so she could fix it herself. Said her daddy was a mechanic. Fixed the rear end / differential on it herself — with just a little help from a friend to drill out a sheared bolt. *Don't you get cold?* I asked. *Naw, I gotta' old quilt to wrap around me when I drive. I'm just happy it starts.*

That's three cents

I was a Frontenac, Kansas bootlegger
every 4th of July back in the mid 1960s.
Cherry Bombs, Bulldogs and M-80s hidden
under the 1 X 12 pine counter that displayed
Black Cats, parachutes, bottle rockets,
Lady Fingers, snakes, sparklers,
and assorted nightworks.
All surrounded by 2 X 4s and chicken wire
with a tin roof. Built it myself.
Great location – at the intersection where
Highway 160 turns north on its way
to the Missouri state line – directly across
from Sam Cicero's filing station, and its small town scenes
played out between clangs of the pneumatic black hose.
Locals sat in their cars like sultans as Sam hurried out
from the hoist where he was changing oil,
wiping his hands on a red shop rag, saying, *Filler up?*
She's high-test ... aaand antiknock ... aaand taylor made
by Senator Kerr and Mr. McGee. The famous Kerr-McGee.
Then, as he popped the hood, *Check your water,*
oil aaand battery water at the same time?
This was followed by spirited Q. and A.
about work, family, ballgames, etc.
as he circled from pump to hood and back.
Around two in the afternoon it would get to be about
110 degrees under the tin roof, so I'd grab a dime
out of the cigar box I used to make change,

walk over to Sam's, pull a NuGrape from the jaws
of the horizontal Pepsi cooler, and head back
as Sam called over my shoulder,
Aaand don't forget to bring back the bottle, Jay.
That's three cents.

sunday

old pickup idling
om, om, om, om, om, om, om,
my meditation

*

three white puffs of cloud
low angling north, fast and pure
oh baby, baby

*

at sunday service
young preacher / old testament
no room for jesus

*

deep in the ozarks
monks silent in the abbey
their mojo working

*

afternoon snowfall
in st. mary's parking lot
young priest does doughnuts

Caryn Mirriam-Goldberg

Getting Started

seems easy as the chickadee perched
on the swing set in the storm

until the first long downward dog,
the arms searching for solace,

the breath too short on the inhale,
staccato on the out breath,

the lungs fluting memory and forecasts,
the heart amplifying the pulse,

until you bend your knees and sink to the ground
like a black colt in the moon grass.

Can you remember the lightness of no effort?
Did it ever happen, will it ever happen again

like birds landing on gutters, like rain the grass drinks,
like the easy sidewalk shadowed by yellow iris

a world unfolding all directions in the sunlight?

The Yoga of Memory

Let the body elongate each breath and dream.
What's hurting has its own low notes.
Let the heat exhale, the chill encompass.

Let come the picture of a car parked on the shoulder,
orange berries hanging from thorny branches,
telephone wires etched in sunlight, having arrived
from the past to show the future even this is a gift,
just like the startle of the cold pond last August
when you were afraid to go further,
but the water called, and so you did.

Or that night in her father's convertible, up and down
hills in the Ozarks, topless in wind that poured thick
and variegated, Queen Anne's Lace to the right,
the yellow line ahead, as you drove into the rising moon.

Dusk filled your body then, as it does now.
Exhale. Evening swoops down outside
of how you make time.

Stand up and walk this miracle home.

Finding the Fire (Tapas)

for Anne

Start with the toes, how they grip the mat,
then lift to balance the sky of your streaming words
dissolving in the fresh air.

Start with nothing but mild exhaustion,
a headache, a warehouse of excuses,
someone else's shawl falling off your shoulders.

Start with a slip of paper from an old fortune cookie
that says, *not what you expected.*

Start with whatever small will remains to try again,
knowing you will fail and fall, but welcoming the effort.

Start with wind rushing the windows. Start with
the breath, ragged because it's too hard to hold the pose,
you never could do this, and *this* changes the shape
of your story about a girl getting lost.

Love the art of losing things as well as the hard-won
resistance of your sore legs as you bend your knees
to sit in the middle of the air.

Whatever fire sparks in your body is enough
as the humidity of the room loosens the old skins
of what you could never do, even if you shiver
and almost fall asleep long before svasana.

Start with the beginning of this glimpse.

Gnarled, Weathered, and Worn by Glory Benacka

Roy Beckemeyer

In Search of a Word

—Sonnenizio after a line from Mark Jarman's "Unholy Sonnet"

In their sheer numbers, motes of dust ride, clinging—
motile on the breaths of long-dead bards:
like letters, *mots,* phrase-fragments, words like shards
from books, or notes from a motet—singing,

soaring. You'd swear they are a living motif—
their motive to course shafts of sunlight,
to calm emotions, settle, alight
on books from which voices emote a sheaf

of language—words of pedestrian, motorist,
politician, poet—motivate
us to eliminate rote. Motivate
us to open tomes, find the *mot juste*—to list

the word specific, exact, out of all those motes—
the one motion-captured speck perfection wrote.

Tactical Sonnet

To place these words and thoughts and rhymes just so
reminds me of the games that I once played—
arranging soldiers made of lead in rows,
in regimental colors, all arrayed.

To build a sonnet there's a strategy—
not one that's found in Sun Tzu's *Art of War*—
but a prosodic sort of pageantry:
pentameter, a rhythmic repertoire.

The iambs and the trochees march along,
metrical soldiers, foot-troops, every one.
Upbeats and downbeats will propel the song
until enjambment ends a line — it's

done. To use a military metaphor,
First, win the sonnet battle, then the war.

Dsyfunctional

...not a man for farming, say the fields...
—Ted Kooser, "Abandoned Farmhouse"

His harvest: a bumper crop of heartaches;
aspirations tilled under, row after
dusty row; no children's warming laughter;
rusted tractor, dull plow, broken-tined rake;

wife and helpmate's love withered by this drought;
his dry-face grim, gray as the leaning barn;
weed-tangled thoughts that missed signs that warned,
omens that marked him: failed, feckless lout

of a farmer, yokel, oaf, debtor, clod,
broken-axled, flat-tired, fractured man,
ground down so far that he no longer can
attempt to endure, to carry on. *God*

help me, he mumbles into a deaf wind,
steps off the hay loft; sows his final sin.

Brian Daldorph

Seven Days

Monday you've still got half a bottle
of vodka left over from Sunday,
plus half a jug of poppy-seed tea.
Should get you through to Tuesday.

Tuesday you call your doctor's office and beg
for an appointment with Dr. Grace.
You tell her your back pain's killing you—
she gives you a prescription to get rid of you.

Wednesday you're hurting and you have only two pills left
and the collection agency keeps calling about bills
you'd forgotten about. You call Jimmy, ask for credit:
You shitting me? You know the rules.
You find five dollars in a drawer
and go buy a bottle of gut-rot.

Thursday Iris comes over with a little bag of whiteness
she wants to share with you
because she's scared to do it alone.
You turn on Velvet Underground.
You don't have to wait for your man.

Friday you are waiting for your man
after selling the TV set your mother bought for you
because she thought it would be *company.*
You're waiting for Jimmy
who's never early, he's *always* late.

Saturday you are tired of this shit and decide
to clean up your act, really clean it up
get back to keeping fit, the way you used to do it.
You run three blocks then crawl back
and use the rest of the stuff from Jimmy.

Sunday you find a stash of poppy seeds and get busy
making tea because Sunday afternoons always hurt
and if you can only make it to Monday
then everything's open for business again.

Afterwards

I don't think about her. I don't miss her,
I do not. I do not. I have plenty
without her, my friends and my family—
though I don't often see them anymore.
There's an assumption that someone on his own
is a sad, lonely man
yet I feel more alone with people all around.
I've often sat with neighbors, friends
listening to them talk about things I don't know:
Alaska, the price of onions, where to go
next vacation, Paris or Rome. I do not miss her, no.
At night I walk in new snow and stop
surprised I have made footsteps.

Arrival

I slide a single sheet of paper to the clerk:
That's about the sum of my life, I say.
The clerk glares at me: *That's all you've got?*
That's just about it. I had a pretty small life.
Birthdate, death date, a bit about education,
jobs, family, my book on bees,
my self-published cookbook.
The few friends I'd have died for.
You know that most people submit a ton
of paperwork, certificates, letters, shopping lists,
official documents, newspaper cuttings, notes
and this is all you've got?
This is it, I say. *Everything apart from this*
I could take or leave so I left it behind. She looks at me
like I'm trouble, then ticks a few boxes.
Take a seat in the waiting room.
He will see you soon.

Stephen Johnson

Invocation to John Brown

You're hanged well, John Brown, and the only one
With that ox-eyed stare right out of King James. That rust
In your beard is blood reefed on the wine-

Red plains of Kanzas. Frothed and snagged, you fist
Scripture from your lungs in fiery reverend cant.
Who's to interpret your rent tongue? You're last

And first John who gospeled in Kanzas: the saint
Excoriating brute flesh with an ox-hide strop,
The penitent Jeremiah bent

On raising New Babylon. Your vision: Rip
America's slag-wasted body into pure
Hosannas; smelt the God-less dross; keep

His will hammered until the States curl over
Like Christ's nailed hands. Work of the devil, child of God,
This is my invocation to the grave: Sear

The Word into my skull. Brand the brain *DEAD,*
Relieved of guilt, Osawatomied, and penned
Like pigs in your tin can-of-sass heart. Bleed

Fear and decency, and I'll understand
Your anthraxed rant. No, we will go together down
In your Sodomized heart, together sound

the Marais de Cygne night, dark like us, one in sin.

goat drinks a little gin in mid-afternoon and prevaricates

And if his offering be a goat, then he shall
offer it before the Lord.
—Leviticus 3:12

i'm a beast   a goat
a piece of meat
with a shaggy coat
an animal   a brute

unwilling   to reason
to try that treason
which tempts a man
to know   to want

all   the same as sane
can be   a kid's need
of milk   and blood
drunk   like me
                        split-
hoofed
            i eat rubber and tin
i pay for all but one
                        sin

Invective Concerning Wayward Anglers

It is truly living luxury. Might as well be staying at
the Radisson Meuhlbach.
The skillet's greased and the Coleman stove's waiting
to be fired up in the morning for poor-man's eggs.
I got the tent up, boat in, and two lines wet already,
and here comes some silly son of a bitch with his son
of a bitch son fishing my water.
The boy just finished off a Shasta Root Beer and bear
claw, tossed the can rattling in the boat. His pop
should have explained by the time sonny boy here
was two that bass spook easy. This water won't be
good to fish again until next July, and here it is
September. So you tell me. What would you do?
Now I know you understand how I hope this breacher
of good fishing etiquette has more sons and daughters,
how I wish they all grow up to be fine, fine carp fisher-
men and creek noodlers, and how I pray when they
finally, finally cast their last bait upon the waters,
their bodies shall sink to the bottom of a DDT'd farm
pond good for nothing but watering two-headed cows.
May copperheads wrap about their limbs.
May bottomfeeders pluck that silly-ass look out of
their sockets. And may this man's children never know
water, never know how it levels everything, above and
below.

But this boy, this boy I do wish the very best.
May his liver never rot from a daily twelve-pack
of Olympia.
May he be the prodigal son and develop a real talent
for cutthroat trout and sockeye salmon.
May nothing but clean-water fishing fill his days.
May he travel far—Montana, Washington, Alaska,
and farther still—far from Kansas, far from this
fishing hole.
May he wade streams gracefully, cast skillfully with
line strong and flies true.
May he luck into a record Chinook, and in that instant,
oh, in the very moment of the perfect hook, may he
splash blindly into a family of feeding Grizzlies.
May he come face to muzzle with the legitimate
claim on that hole.
May he be crushed and ground into a tasty pâté.
And may his father never know of his son's fortune,
good and ill.

The man with his boy gives me a wave.
Naturally, I touch the bill of my cap, say,
What are they biting on?

Burnt Prairie Paths by Glory Benacka

Dennis Etzel, Jr. / Kevin Rabas

Summer Storm

my other mother passed away sooner than we thought
after years with struggling with lightning bolts
of death a surprise

like the next night's thunderstorm in the midst
of high-nineties days she was a surprise
in my post-father post-trauma summer

spent as wheels on a bicycle dodging dogs
who came after me through those cursed months
named after Roman emperors

as harsh as a father's rule until
she carried microbursts of books of music
a peace with downpours for relief

—DE,Jr

With a Stick

If I were on your block
when I was young, I'd be
a littler kid, but one
unafraid of dogs, come
with a stick, help
you get by, help you
down the block
and into the field.

—KR

I Lived in the New Mutants Comic Book Issues Eighteen through Thirty During Middle School

in a mansion where every safety was given to me
even in the danger room a haven
where the alien fugitive runs to

away from his father several asylums in
these rooms I placed my own walls up
as dreams told me something dangerous would come

if only I could only stay here. I lived in issues
eighteen through twenty not just for three months
but for years after middle school I visited the mansion

days full of safety in this naive haven fleeing
my father like an alien the stranger granted no asylum
I stayed in these rooms here told myself the danger

passed yes those issues I could pass through I lived
with the new mutants as I was a mutant who lived
in the trees of mansions my powers of teleportation

I believe in relocation as I think back on those
strangers who came to build a home all asylums
granted I believe in every dream here

to fight a father who sees people as children
builds walls to send actual children away
walls I wish I had mutant powers to vanish

—DE,Jr

Cycle Broken

I can't know
what it was
in Bud's house
at the end of the street, how he
came at me one day, fits up,
chest out, eyes like hot coals,
and I flipped him in the grass
and even lent a hand up.
He called me "karate cricket"
after that, but I know
at home Bud's Dad also
put up fists, or slammed them down,
or put them into the table
or the side of Bud's face. Bud came
at me wanting something back,
something back from the world, the block,
the other kids. My father's father
used his fists. My mother said,
Not with him.

—*KR*

Chip on the Shoulder

Tony taught me the meaning
behind the cliché when he dared

me I replied I will not knock that
off I will not knock that off even

my father would yell at me
knock it off from the other room

I froze unmoving to a fight
except for one time my punches

fired from my fists I apologized
years later to Jason but he said no

he didn't remember me being a bully
but the times we stayed nights over

at each other's houses playing Atari
through early morning screens

firing cannons or dodging ghosts
we kept the volume down as low

as we could stay quiet knowing
our respective fathers watched

in the darkness of another room
full of beer of silence waiting for someone

to break the rules so we kept our shoulders
clear and to the floor

—DE,Jr

At the Sleep Over

In the dark, Rick's dog
jumps, lunges,
and bites Dave, and Rick's Dad
hops out in his underwear,
tighty-whiteys, bear
hugs that dog, its teeth
red with Dave's skin, and we know
life can also be
tooth & claw, tooth
& claw.

—KR

Kevin W. Peery

Morning Moon

This
mourning
Moon
accentuates
the
timberline...
as
my
gin
soaked
eyes
play
tricks...

And
ancient
spirits
shape
shift...
beyond
the
orchard
bench
terraces...

Where
this
fresh
blood
trail
will
help
guide
them...
to
all
that's
left
of
me

Bentonia to Bonnaroo

I'll never forget
the night
we drove
Luther's
dove gray
Lincoln
from Bentonia
to Bonnaroo...

I got all
twisted up
on Ancient Age...
listenin' to
Jimmy Reed
singin'
Kansas City
Baby...

Not knowin'
the next day...
would be
the last time
I'd ever hear
Burnside play
the *Death*
Bell Blues

Splattered Gray Matter

Is honesty
really
the best
policy...
when everyone
already knows
you're
a goddamn
liar...

Like a
wise man
from Waco
once said –

Never play
Russian roulette
with an
automatic....

Sure…
the cold
hard truth
might set
ya free...

But the
odds are
certainly
against
a misfire...

And
what kind of
sick son of a bitch
gets his kicks
scoopin' up
the splattered
gray matter
of a lyin' man
anyway

Flying Dreams by Annie Macker

Patricia Traxler

How to Tell if You're Possessed
(and what to do about it if you are)

Go home immediately and eat something raw;
watch for sweet absurdity and visible decay.
Court silence. Turn out the lights and walk
from room to room. Do not attempt
to go for help; do not attempt to pray.
Speak to nothing that can transubstantiate.

Move gingerly to the end of the hall and open
the door you kept closed. Remove your clothes.
Enter, then turn like a dancer in the dark room.
Spin, spin, stop. Open your mouth and turn again,
slowly swallowing your God's eternal indifference.
Now wrap yourself in his immense silence; float

Just above the surface of your own singing skin.
Migrate to the farthest edge of sleep, breathing
deeply in, out, in; open your eyes as wide as you can
behind their glistening lids. If you talk in your sleep
now, you are possessed. If you are if you are you
will live the way dreams live on within us, hovering
at the peripheries of knowing, beginning again
and again and again and then fading away.

October Grackles

Hundreds of you, everywhere above me,
lining every branch of every tree,
you own the day. I can't love you.
Go, leave my elms and oaks, ash
and cottonwoods; continue on your way,
sharp voices etching pure October air.

You need only yourselves, your song
and propaganda. I understand this.
Once, I was like you, craving change and stir,
the momentary fancy. And then I was here,
where place became time. Now, give me back
the stillness, please, and I will give you this:
Hurry, leave, before you lose the will to fly.

The Deer

In darkness beside the empty road he must have
waited and then, drawn by the approaching light,
in a microsecond he's leapt from the shelter
of cottonwoods into the swath of my beams. I hear
and feel the impact, see him in profile arcing
upward, illuminated, hooves antlers hooves he
tumbles, amber eye opened wide and fixed on this
moment, his own sense of the world we share.

Stopping my crumpled car on the verge beside
a stand of cottonwood, oak, and blood-red sumac,
I see him in a heap across the road, look away,
make myself look back again. Then a slash of light,
truck pulling in behind my car. Someone wanting to
help, maybe. The man comes to my window, waves
a hand at the carcass, two of his fingers missing.

Are you going to eat the deer? he asks. By killing
a living creature, have I made it my own to give? I shake
my head, but then behind the man I see the deer lifting
his head and in a long moment, struggling to his feet
while the man waits for my answer. The deer staggers,
then bounds into the woods beyond the road. The man
notes my gaze and turns. *Goddammit,* he says. *Fuck.*

Without another word he lopes back to his truck. His headlights come on again, illuminating my car's interior. my hands still on the wheel. I watch him take the road, disappear. The wind returns and cottonwoods stir. What other life might be waiting, hidden beneath rough boughs in darkness? The engine hesitates, then catches. Enclosed in buckled metal, I move back onto the road, watching shadows and shapes along the edge for signs of life.

Joel Matthews

Separatists and Loyalists on the Native Prairie

Pete Seeger once said: *Lawyers change old laws to*
fit new citizens.
The nicks and cuts on my hands are a bloody witness
as I engage the fence
        new posts, stronger posts, taller posts
        new-fangled barbed wire
        and fencing pliers with scriptural eloquence.

The old fence line was for cattle, mainly Angus
it was rusty and wobbly in spots
and orioles snatched long hairs from the barbs-
        a strange harvest from a ubiquitous line.
To put herds in little boxes seemed the right thing.

It's not always greener on the other side
separatists and loyalists jeer
        through the electrified galvanized razor-
wired monstrosity
singing the same music as the democrats and
republicans
        the imperialists and the isolationists
        the red-necks and the hippies
        the Sunni and the Shia
        us and them
        me and you.

All on the same ground with only a line between,
        a line fashioned by our own hands
        only heretics and traitors cross.
The burden of engaging the fence in combat is valliant
those who take shrapnel in their flesh
those drug through the streets
those who sit at the front of the bus.
I really don't mind the nicks and cuts on my hands
        stains gathering at my feet
it's all the same stained ground with only a line between.

The New and Improved Neanderthal

Us, we modern ones
hunt for the closest parking spots
and fill our carts with name brand, not generic goods.
We pay the dues of hides, shiny stones,
and pretty feathers
with the deft wave of a Master Card key fob
encoded with DNA imprint sequences
and retinal scans.

We cerebral Cro Magnons
litter the veld with constructed caves
with central cooling machinery
and a stocked wine cooler
(each bottle captured live in the wilds).
Cave paintings now called abstract art
represent a most distorted story of the hunt
and visions of the shaman.

The spear of point and click
is effortless hunting, sitting-down hunting.
Easily caught is the prey of a neoprene chin-strap
to stop me from snoring,
a new mate,
enrollment in a subversive parochial movement,
and epic stories of time-bending neutrinos, winking
electrons, and the space between.

All easily caught, passive prey.

Some of us used to excel with gazelles,
but now hunt the popular vote
or the revered greenback.

Us sly sapiens
hunt the most bizarre of beasts
gather the most bizarre goods
and gazelles are still
gazelles.

parcel

Buddha came through the mail today
in a flimsy box
the postmaster had no celebration for the event
    no sand paintings in the language of
    symbolism
    no prayer flags fluttering
    no bringing together of the hands nor bowing
    not even a simple Namaste
    just a flimsy box
    a plain flimsy box
        no fancy labels
        no foreign tongue
        no warnings of fragility and no gaudy
        stamps of insurance values
        and conditions thereof

a plain flimsy box
that was, as it seems it should be,
a bit lop-sided
one side heavy:
    to remind me of the dead wood in my life
one side light:
    to remind me of how things can be
and just as it should be:
    to remind me of the perfection

I suspect some prophets
travel only in First Class
        their posh private jets
        instant feed satellite connections
        rare exquisite wines
        priceless trappings galore
        and an entourage of sycophants groveling
        something about not being worthy

Buddha came
from that plain flimsy box
a bit dusty,
just like the rest of us in this real life
as it should be

Cal Louise Phoenix

Relics

For Bevel…

An ache is a petrol boost—not unlike
the weight of these cannons
resting where
our bones have molded into shipsides.

This boy and I had insides
on which we sailed: a swamp
of antique leaves and an alien's blue.
We drank each other from curly straws
swung matching mugs
and slurred from balcony points—it's the place

where we met and now visit
through a weak soup
a year and seven months too late.

We were meant to go ashore
on a postcard. It was done
once I comforted his belly with a drunk beetle

once he'd made me a believer
returning the favor underwater.

I discovered something holy then
in the third hour of the fifth morning
in the arch of my spine

in the writing in the sand—it's the place
where I've piled an altar
and now visit with tucked skirts
a year and five months too late.

Like a moth in horizon paints
he was swallowed by landscape.
My anchor was his request
the counter tilt of the wheel—transplanted
to a beach of dust and melted drywall.

Whisper-sung in an earthworm's breath
a clasp is my hymn:

Come, aim, boy. Light the fuse, boy. Hallelujah.

After Seven O'clock

That summer sweltered as hot and wet
as the mouths they mashed together
to keep the wrong words from forming.
While he laid floors in cut-offs held up with rope
she listened to Mozart and collected butts
in failed ceramic projects.
The bent blinds and kneaded carpet whispered
of wanting—waiting until his truck belched
to a halt below the balcony.

Of parks and porches, they slapped bugs
scratched bites, and threw handfuls of sweat
from their brows and backs. In his shed, amongst
the smell of spoiled milk and cat piss, his knife-like hips
ground her mid-drift into cream.
After the humming had dissipated,
those bruises became welcomed company.

Before the string snapped (under breast, between ribs)
ten months unfolded. In the drunk cold, it happened:
    the calloused guitar cracking
    and carpenter's hand narrowed a finger
    from shelves to boxes, from the door
    to the trunk of her car.

When her feet began to drag, he carried her
back to bed for a final tumble
before putting her out on the porch like a stray,
where she surveyed the frost and grime
for a place to call *home.*

Growing up to ignore the spoon-shaking direction
of her father *(Watch out for those boys*
—the ones from the country) she gathers what she deserves:
        a backside of red and purple ribbons
        and the strain of an empty bottle,
        where she might have held her pride before.

Overcast

a calendar means to pine by every square
—those aching seasons float by on notes of old words
for a year, *I think my brain might fall out*

the farmhouse has settled into disrepair:
dust veils the poetry scrawled walls my cookware
weeds have eaten our garden—those crops
abandoned to rot

and yet, upstairs I stay
sitting on the master bed
plucking webs as they collect from my eyelashes

and wear our fantasy like a shadow
though it bleeds to ripple my draperies
with a sticky shame that
keep my wrists and tongue in captivity

The Owl, Pussycat & Three Blind Mice by Annie Macker

Melvin Litton

OLD LIVES

I.

A subtle existence upon the wold,
the wolf knows loneliness the same as
an old woman. My orchard bears fruit,
but with an agony of thorns on the cross,
a painful birth and is always so…

A savage of middle night and morning
cloaked in flannel instead of mammal skins,
I count no coups, merely thoughts.
A serpent possessed of fine poison,
yet no fangs for delivery. My life tragically
moored with the worms beneath the sun.
No fields, nor beasts, only my labor to sow,
I harvest forms spiced with color
and variance of emotions, like storms,
and lastly, death. I await spring and new
blood, and a sword to battle the adversity
which shadows like a brother…

And in the East, to the valley of all origin,
where night and morning wed beneath the
physics of evolution, the day unfolds. But with
insufficient heat to move this flesh whose passions
wane and still. Empty, I flee the feist of present-time

to confront the terrible specters caterwauling from
the past, where each word is voiced in the rapt,
vertiginous speech of those whose light
has long faded beyond the curtain…

II.

The wind seeks new borders,
flees the steppe warriors of the North
to settle its wings upon the lees
and timber of my valley…

It rains unseen…
Diaphanous mists drift over fields where
angry ghost fog hangs haunting the gullies
like white death of cannons fired in silence,
while beyond, through the bottoms, hay bales
lay ungathered like soldier lads at Antietam…

It rains unseen…
A moist, vaporous breath enfolds, clogging the
distance, the scene contained, entranced, mystic.
Here a Red-tail Hawk rolls and searches,
mesmerizing through the liquid sky.
Colors deep like water, of dimension,
geometry, and hue, their essence ensconced
in finite grays, browns, yellows, russets, and
greens, like leaves in Appalachian coal towns.

Umber silhouettes soften the angles while
burnt grass and rotted wood incense the hollows.
The entire scene painted in muted oils and lacquered
mists as if imported like the pheasant from Asia to
bestow ancient riches and metaphor…

It rains unseen…
In the rude evening hogs rut and feed,
stirring mud and feces like in a Spanish still-life
where peasants stomp their feet in vatted grapes…

Dusk deepens like lines of ink
writhing across the page as the night fox
emerges from crevices of the dark, sculpted land.
Now the moon serves witness to the lowly shadow
of the sun and through the window I perceive
the ghost image of a candle and rush
to my old friend, the fire, who comforts me
with stories of Old Lives on the long savannahs
and cold tundras of lost history…

III.

With thoughts of winter I climb the stairs
to search quilted warmth instead
of cool sheets and sex…

Yet tonight my mistress sleep yields no pleasure,
leaves me longing for her semblance at the window.

I turn from her cold eyes and walk the darkness
as the wick flame illumines my passage
and sets the furtive shadows dancing.
Outside, the moon whispers veiled light,
the hand that holds it forth forever hidden
like the distance through the rain…
Why to the heavens plead?
Why should infinity beckon one
Whose utter origins stalk each breath?
The mystery that buoys the moon and suspends my life,
to what end? That I should lie alone and supine,
a corpse, a cool light, my flesh eclipsed with the owl and
serpent, death rendering all forms into the same pale
sculpture?

Time-scorned, mocked, so that my progeny should one
day visit my bones and call to me:

Old Skullman! Still and silent warrior!
You suffer the delirium of too much sleep…

And further presume of me with callow intellect:

What colored visions danced within?
Were you medieval or Neolithic man?
Were you soldier or scholar?
Did knowledge abound in that cavity?
Were you a brooding man, insular and heroic,
scarred by wounds of inner battle, leaving long
gashes furrowed upon your brow and bloodstains
beneath your eyes? Did you stare in common with

the idiot and drunkard, the crippled and feeble,
share their admonition and rejection,
their shame and tragedy? Did you cry and curse
at the mass adulation of fools? Were you poet,
prophet, or beggar…or a prince of fools?

Did that two-faced goddess, Reason, the one of
golden hair, take your youth and teach you the
laws of pleasure, of arrogant gain, bravado, and
senseless quests? Did she have you lusting for the
knowledge of her flesh then abandon you for one
younger and of fatter purse?
Tempting, jealous, frivolous, and haughty, did
she redden your eyes and leave you stumbling
blind, begging redemption?
Skullman! Old mystery!
If you could speak, what words would echo
from the ether's lexicon?

You child, talk to me of madness and existence?
You wade shallow waters and I have swum with
leviathan. Spirits are not new to me…

IV.

To the Northwest, perilous drums of violent
summer rains rumbled as lowering disquietudes
which augured tornadoes echoed from the South.
The sun stroked the panorama, knelling
beneath Red Cloud's mighty arm while

Mankato's thunderous spirit stormed in nemesis
over the land.
Mankato! Red Cloud! Near and mythic, I was born
amid reverberations of their ghostly warring…

In winter, stalked cane leaned tee-peed
in the fields, snow-skins of white buffalo
covering the sheaves to shed the cold
from my inner warmth where
I squatted in savage peace…

And nights beneath the summer's purple
sky, vertigo induced by the fathomless depths,
dizzied by the avid pull of oceanic beauty and death,
my heart unbidden by sorrow grasped the infinite, my
spirit certain. I harvested fireflies in the evenings,
their illuminations another cosmos.
The gods reigned the heavens, and I the earth…

But it happened, as happens with all.
Suddenly the door to the wind sprung open
and my questions could no longer be answered…

I lay in a glen of young elms, their swaying
shoots anchored in the moist May soil, and
watched feathery clouds whiff overhead, traced
by sun-tinted swallow wings. I teased yet feared
the shadow man who stood beyond the barn,
appearing midway after lunch and before the call
to dinner, then grew the full span towards the creek
and became the night. I climbed the sapling elms

and sailed against zealous winds, an unwary child
about to fall and receive broken dreams…

Since that day I have chased shades of beauty,
flesh, and poetry, luckless as a fiddle without a bow…

No longer have I the gaiety of a lark,
though I wish, nor the certitude of a young
and fallow mind. The philosopher's mastery
of situations, his acrobatics with past, future,
and distance, no – nor a mathematician's grasp
of vague, ineffable calculus. Madness eludes me,
intuition I distrust, leading more often to chaos.
The elliptical yo-yoing of conversation bores me.
And religion would damn me to fits of sanctity
and shame. I haven't the courage to say
"I do," nor sufficient guilt to confess "I did."
So what is there to hold me but the will
of music, magic, and woman?

V.

As the moon and her influence visit the dun
wood an incessant pulse gnaws at my fingertips
to caress my guitar and hatch the yolk of melody.
Upon the dappled wall my vision defines an apparition
that claws and chants of abeyant forms.

My calloused fingers hunger for their prey
like a wolf pack searching through the far night,

wanting the other, the nameless, to receive its
pitch and grace...

A stallion softly neighs across the pasture.
My flesh is warmed. Four and twenty years I
have walked the earth, yet part of me has slept,
that which is born bereft, the orphaned soul
of each generation...

I have slashed through jungles and clove waters
of the Aegean, marched with Roman legions,
and fallen in the desert. I've bled my life into the
Tigris and the Mississippi, roamed the valleys of Crete
and Kansas, and fled the night of a hundred separate
centuries...

Always in moments of love I have such visions...

And who is not my father?
Is not all substance an experience of itself?
Honey its sweetness; the mind its thought,
and all thoughts mere ideas of sweetness, cold, sorrow,
delight, the whole gathered like driftwood on a beach
for the flaming pyre to disseminate through measure of
ocean, continents, and space?
We bear the time-print of all origin, genetics of
fantastic depth, nebular birth and galactic wounds, the
mineral asters of Precambrian seas, exuberant fruit of
the Pleistocene, of reptilian obsessions, devils, gods,
creatures of Dostoyevsky, warriors of Stonehenge and
the Crusades. Beneath the sanguine sky and fathoms of

death surfaces again and again,
no matter how faint the last attenuated cry,

"Must live, must live, must live..."

Who is not my father?

I reach into my gut to seek the future, gripping each
moment as it occurs, that the potentialities of moon
and demon, this pitiable flesh and nothingness be
experienced and metaphysically endured, that the lost
wax of visual divinities be granted the finality
of bronze. I stand within this ghost land of fleeting
atmospheres inhabited solely by native cedar masking
the stone and iron-fenced plots of our fathers' graves,
that this twilight be made known and charted,
for it is in the gut that vignettes of mind and heart merge
and are threshed beneath the milestone of sleepless
nights and labored days, producing the narrative of
hidden forces, dark mysteries of the moon's lost surface,
and the shared veins of blood, sperm, spleen, and soil
marking the inheritance of the human soul...

VI.

A lone figure within the diorama of night,
Saturnine with pains of mortality, life's nexus,
and this frigid flesh, this impotence that binds
the dust of our unborn, calling wild yet mute,
drawn to the cool light, the shadow of our earth,

drawn into a sea of storms, this cavity that bears
no child save silence…

A single breaker moistens Africa's bony shore.
The wind rustles then rests, breathless, captive
in lapsed ballon. Autumn returns the self to my
flesh as dawn transcends opacity with a gray,
monochrome translucence that advances
briefly then awaits…

The night's contagious richness stills the sun's
ingress as the heart ingests motes of song
refracted through all memory. Focused on this
temporal plane, a spirit seemingly risen from
an old borrow, a ruin of stone, its brumal breath
formed in echo of my father's birth, an animism
chorused in rivers, clouds, and fiery coals…

As scents of old tributaries become
known again at flood stage, fruits from
thickets and arbors caught in its savage grip,
so the quintessence of unrecalled ancestry
answers the saturation of our mortal currents

and a man becomes the cynosure as his soul rages above
blood tide, more sentient than perfervid flesh, battling a
maelstrom of unveiled reflections…

A cognitive presence imbues my shadow's form,
a tangential vernacular evolving at the periphery of
consciousness, an avatar which is and is not the self…

From the East I journeyed, frail
substance upon a long, shadowed
path glazed by sun and dew, seeking
my shadow as a virgin seeks promise.
For a moment I stood achieved, the
polestar of creation, a triumph brief
and deceiving, for my substance and
energies soon waned. I journeyed West,
again seeking my shadow cast behind,
growing long and mysterious within
the vesperal cloak until that greater
shadow consumed my substance...

Vain embers of anxiety flare in my heart,
this message a vile anchor to the vessel of
my thoughts: Am I not the pilgrim returned
from Mecca via the river Acheron, transfixed
by dire knowledge of our shared demise?
Of fate I expect nothing but the life of a
flameless dragon, hunted and haunted.
The weeds will grow tall upon my grave...

You are Narcissus crying wolf,
frightened of burning life and age,
a fool to long for immortality of form
over substance, ignorant of deities
within your reach. Gods subject to
age and death, yet gods no less.
And of your father's memory
you are ignorant as well.
Look! The sun is risen!

Its hand brings forth the seed of life,
awakens moist, wanton procreation,
and forms the trees, great bones of
fibrous statuary, to commemorate the
ancient coupling of flesh and spirit.
The pollen of your life falls unwedded
beyond the flower and fails to fructify
like an incubus cast out of dreams.
Wonder that Dionysian blood should anger
and boil within lax Lutheran flesh?
This quandary of submissiveness, leave it!
The only certain death is life suborned,
shamed, and subdued...

The damp, lethargic night cowers aside
the stallion's celerity as the aura of ancient
amplitudes forms the morning's first light.
I cast my last draught of energy into its
opulent wave like a harpoon into Leviathan,
seeking to rein in my mad inertia and doubt,
forsaking the night, cruel mistress, my sleepless
soliloquy, for the day, to explore a further river
and vision and there discern a path...
The wind cries through the crannies,
depositing tremolos of old madrigals,
probing the senses with intoxicants
and reckless wonder...
I surrender like a savage entering
the Sun Dance, receiving in its entirety
the half-vision that has haunted me since
I was a child...

His face glows with lines of vibrant
poetics haloed by the pale ochre of
memory, his brow etched by tragedy
and long experience of a visceral heart,
his undulant voice expressing now the
thunder, now the gentle patter of the rain.
Old as a Druid and mutable as a flood,
his lineage as much of the sea as the prairie,
his hands in the mold of a dayworker or peasant,
the Irish, German, night and wolf, warm his blood.

He is a Nordic ghost, a Cheyenne son,
the timeless beast whose source and border
lies beyond and within that part of each
which falls to the soil and rises in the seed,
which survives self-murder to enter the life of a son,
which haunts the gibbet and crossroad,
paring agony from one flesh to another
as the wind carries eluvium and desecration
to regions of innocence...

Call him Old Lives, the culminated longings
And passions of a species, our fervent memory
scintillating off snow mountains and far deserts,
man returned to self and soul,
progenitor of unresolved poetry...

Harley Elliott

Medicated

When you're home alone
and all fucked up
there are no questions
only answers.

Of course let us
lie down here with the
lion and the lamb
since we're all in
this together and
anything is possible.

You could go out
to the curb and wave
your junk like a flag.
Everyone would understand
and the answer
to what could be
simpler is nothing.

You take your meds
and existence breaks
down to the framework
when men first made
Eve the patsy.

Oh there are dues
to be paid your
bathrobe flaps and
your slippers agree.
Clearly the one hundred
percent solution
is global love.

Politics and all the
silly isms will be
sorted out once
we scrape the
scales from our eyes.
Yes we can work this out.

But love must start somewhere
and you appoint yourself
the prime mover.
You make a note
to smile at the mailman.
World peace. No lie.
But then suddenly
it's time for bed.

The Yodeling Joker

He gangbustered into town
and all the stoplights died.
Just to show he was serious
he licked the color
out of the sunset
and tied a knot in the wind
or said he did.
The powerhouse took note

but they were yodeled
into a headlock trance
and soon were voting
for a chimpanzee
in every tree and a
typewriter for every
chimpanzee as well
as inventing fish jello
and garlic cola to sell
to the culturally insecure.

The Republic pulled the
covers over its head
and all the preachers
quickly learned to yodel.
Politicians stayed
home and masturbated.

Cash registers broke
down in tears.
Violins gave up the ghost.
We forgot how to make bread.

He has us in
a kind of thrall the
powers excused themselves
and sold us a lurch
to be left in
and wisdom remained
in no danger
of being discovered.

The Right Dog

To greet peacekeepers
as equals and scout
out approaching evil
give us a dog with
a good nose for intentions

one with plenty of
genetic tangle in
its history and enough
wolf spark to carry
itself as if it belonged
to the world at large.

Let us have a dog who
waits for the right signal
but knows how to play
and when sitting side by
side this dog leans
on you just a little
to let you know.

Michael Cissell

As God Was, America Was,
Say the Butcher Son,

a good idea. So was
the Third Reich, thought
they of the kingdom.
And Israel. Christianity.
Islam. Not to mention
Buddhism. —Shit, Boy, say Bones, many
we is think you bad, son.

Loosen yorself. Look down.
Cross yorself no mo?
What crown up yo
head weigh like dat of Solomon?
Thorns of woe
only one head God gave to carry.
—But think on the chair of Plato

(sunlight in the saddle of
the hill): doesn't matter now
—material or shadow—
what either final cause
each the other was.
—Butcher son, you scares me.
You scares me what you show.

Sunday Morning, Butcher Son Thinks on Salvation

Not in the church I pass on runs.
Not in the litany nor in the storied windows.
Not in the marble stations, nor stiff iconography.
More like a woman full and living.
—Problem Butcher Son is yo thoughts.
Dey should be handled like da ejaculate
of da sweaty Catholic boy—spewed
in da sock and thrown in da wash cause
I knows da indecent filth in yo head
I knows da women sickness bid you run,
will not let you eat, not sleep, not talk
But prevail and work on yo shape, ruin
yo own voice and words bewitched in trance.
Discard da lousy sickness Butcher Son.
Set on yo foot. Reject da offense.
Dispossess da madness and da obstruction.
Like a woman full and living. Fierce and pluck.
Open and charged, fired hot in resolution.
Enduring and universal tremble in my bed.
The vow and communion of heaven and hell
and the sulphurous delight to which I'm lead.

A Deeper Darkness, Say Butcher Son,

Wakes at dawn, or before,
some shapeless panic
like these crows
perched in coffee trees,
like these leaves
heavy between earth and sky,
like this ghost-fog
forming over the lake.
Everything reflects formless

and blurs lives into hydro-imagery.
Like Christ framed mid-ascension
between yesterday and today
and a future nobody exists in.
Like these leaves.
Like these crows.
Between something and nothing
to concretize the dead
and burn away the fog.

Mustang Ghost Dance by Annie Macker

Thad Haverkamp

A Bottle Full of Gideon

And God said, *Let there be.*
So let there be.

Let there be a book full of half-truths
and a bottle, half full of empty promises,
promising full peace.

So let there be,
with a Bible in one hand
and a hand-full of handsome lies
in the other.

And God said.

So let Him Say.
Let Him talk 'till He is blue in the face.

I say.

I say *let there be,*
so let there be.

I say let there be a few more gallons left in the tank,
and a few more miles left under the hood.

I say let the rent check clear,
and let that girl that's smiling be smiling at me.
Let there be one more cigarette left in the pack.

And please, please let that funny, little rash
just be — ringworm?

I say *so let there be.*
So let there be.

But there won't be.

So let Him say what he wants.

Let Him divide day from night.
Let Him command the firmaments and the
waters.

I'll still be stuck here with this book
and this bottle to hear what I have to say.

So let Him keep talking to Himself.

The Way Time Moves Across Asphalt in the Sand Hills of Nebraska

Time takes its time
across the blacktop.

It crosses the low scrub
and patchy dunes
at a pace of its own
determination.

Here Time has nothing but time on its hands,
so it moseys along the Western desert
and gladly yields right-of-way to fence posts
and cattle
and patches of musk thistle.

Time rests
on the center yellow line,
watching the asphalt stretch
from vanishing point
to vanishing point.

Time usually spends its time
ever-rushing forward,
hurtling onward,
rocketing us from the cradle to the grave.

Time flies, in other parts of the world,
but here, in the Sand Hills,
it takes its time.

It watches the lizards
and jackrabbits
and turkey vultures
zip past.

So while the sun waits to exit,
and the moon waits to enter
and I wait for my car to crest the next hill,

Time takes its time
and enjoys the view.

The Man Who Spoke to Ghosts

The Man who Spoke to Ghosts went deaf,

at least that's what he told me
under the bridge
warmed by cheap wine
and Sterno flame.

You know you can't drink that shit to get high
anymore, right? he asked me.

He said it was great being deaf
because the whole world was wound up
neat and tight
in a package
in his head
where it hummed.
Now his ears were locks that kept it all in
and kept the voices out.

The Man who Spoke to Ghosts told me it was
nice to be alone,
for once,
with his red wine
and canned heat
and his own thoughts —
alone without the voices to bother him.

He said the ghosts were tedious and dull,
had no soul,
no life,
nothing interesting to say.

He said they bored the shit out of him
with their constant whining
and carping and pining
for the lives
they once had —
the lives they ignored when they had them.

He took another pull from his bottle,
gave me a slap on the knee,
and told me it was great being deaf.
Finally, a little peace, he said.

Above us the semis
and commuters
and joyriders
rumbled past,
shaking the concrete pillars of his home.
Of course the Man who Spoke to Ghosts heard
nothing.

I opened my mouth to say something
but stopped.
And the Man who Spoke to Ghosts went on
being deaf.

Linda Lewis

Temperance Warrior

With bricks and hatchets, Carry and the Smashers
blasted Kansas saloons like tornadic winds
that whack and splinter, wallop
and fracture.

Often Carry A. Nation crusaded alone, for only she
heard God's charge to demolish dens
of iniquity in Medicine Lodge
and Kiowa.

Six feet tall and calm as a grenadier, she lobbed
a haymaker that unmanned purveyors
and clients who "tarried
at the wine."

She chose a Wichita hotel for its swanky nightclub,
not only bludgeoned fittings and utensils but
slashed the naked lady painting
above the bar.

In Topeka's Senate saloon she clobbered slot machines,
cash register, beer tubing, a barkeep's
composure, the prestige of
senatorial imbibers.

Carry would tip over a keg of ale and cleave it with her
weapon, releasing spume and splash grand as
Old Faithful. (She sold replica hatchets
to go her bail.).

Lillian's Version

That prissy little Quaker trick-shooter was done for.
There, I said it and reckoned it so until Bill Cody
concocted a quarrel, knowing I would up and quit
his Wild West shebang, leave the door open for
Little Miss Sure Shot and her fawning Frank Butler
to waltz right back under the bigtop. That girl sure
didn't cotton to sharing a spotlight. Had a jealous
streak wider than the Mighty Mo. When I showed
up, way younger than Buffalo Bill's female firing
wonder, she scissored years off herself quicker than
you can pluck ticks from a dog's hide. She seen that
Queen Victoria took a shine to Lillian Smith instead
of Annie Oakley, and that rubbed her raw as a
new-laid egg in a Ohio farmyard. Such a show-off:
blam-blam-blamming clay pigeons like champagne
corks popping, blasting ashes off the Kaiser's cigar.
But her shotgun never shattered glass balls like my
Winchester. Show folks can't keep a lid on, so I heard
of her disdain over my flirty ways and fancy duds,
her disgust at my grammar. But I seen it didn't bother
Her Highness Queen Victoria none. My sharpshooting
days are over. My lowdown German artist run off and
left me like my barkeep, lawman and bronc buster.
None of them a stayer like Annie's Frank. I'll give her
that. They say he starved himself after she died. I'm
alone in Bliss, Oklahoma. Just me, and my dogs and
rifles, and some tarnished trophies. In Bliss.
I wonder where Annie Oakley is.

Snakebite

The slitherer that yesterday nipped my toe
took advantage of my naïve belief that it was
safe to traverse from driveway to doorway.
All ten toes — nails cherry painted — were fully
exposed in summer sandals. And I gave no heed
to serpent surveillance. Steps from the car my
ankles were wrapped in coils like those that
clasped Laocoön. The wriggling invader easily
won the bout, offered no signal of remorse,
ate no dust as recompense for his victory.
Thus requited, the narrow fellow glided
among blades and stalks of iris.

Susan Kinney

Snow Melts

The snow has fallen
the shovel and snow-blower
has done the work
moving snow off
sidewalks and driveways
making ways you can walk.

The roads have not
been cleared
cars and truck have
driven over them
making paths
for people to travel.

Traveling in snow
can be hard.

The rows of snow
ripples as the sun
melts the edges.
The puddles are everywhere
it is only January.
Snow edges are around
the sidewalk wet
as snow melts to water.

We Hear It Dripping

The sky pours rain on us
going to the store.
Windshield wipers on the car
cannot get rid of it
every thing is wet.

Shut up in the house
while the weather
wets the ground.
We hear it dripping
off the roof.
It plays a symphony
in our ears.
We try to sleep.

Paint the Room

Green chairs
against green and white walls.
Six pieces of glass reflecting
into the room.
People wearing
clothes of red, blue and yellow
paint the room.

The bearded man
prepares for his speech,
laying out folders,
handing out papers,
with printing on them.

People talk about
writing poetry
inside their
colorful clothes.

A Morning View by Douglas Hoesli

Glory Benacka

The Last Green

In the spring when the green comes there is a sense of relief as life returns. Chartreuse, juniper, sage, olive, emerald, there are so many shades of green. Its many shades express the changing seasons and at the end of each season, before the first frost, there is the last green. By the end, most plants have grown to adulthood, big, tall, and saturated with many shades. It seems like yesterday that they were only seeds, some the size of a spec of sand in your hand. Now they stand proud and tall, but each is approaching its last green. This is the way of things, the natural order is to be born, live, reproduce, and die.

I cried a lot at my Grandma's funeral. Of course, I was sad, that she died, but I was crying a lot extra, because it was the worst funeral I had ever been to. I had never participated in organizing a funeral before, nor had I had a front row seat to death. I suggested we use this portrait of her as a young woman for the obituary, but everyone laughed. The funeral home director suggested that the photo of a 60 year younger woman would make her unrecognizable to those she knew. It was true, one of her best friends said, "who's this" when she saw the portrait on the memorial display. She was memorialized in the newspaper as another gray haired old woman. We all start to look the same before death, no?

My Aunt told me that this was her senior portrait and it turned out so well that my great grandma ordered enough copies for everyone in the family, plus extras. It's truly a well circulated portrait in my family. It is a beautiful portrait, she has a perfect expression of humble beauty and youth. I never knew my Grandma to be vein. In fact she discouraged us from looking at ourselves in the mirror too long as children for fear we would catch some form of shallowness. I obeyed and didn't take to leisurely staring at myself too much. She grew up on a ranch in West Texas and as a rurally cultured woman with a depressionchildhood she had a certain practical sensibility in all things.

For some plants the last green is only for the season, but for others this is their final green. So before the first frost the gardener collects all of the produce even the things that are not ripe yet. Most of it will ripen indoors, it won't be as tasty and fresh, but it will probably get you through November. That first frost kills the last green. We are trying to hold onto that last green, celebrate the end of the season's harvest, and prepare for winter. From that point on brown comes in place of the fading greens in the plants. And we won't see green again for some time.

It's sad, the withering body in the nursing home. When you are just kept comfortable in those last moments in a cinder block room. I cried a lot there too, because it was all so ugly. The artwork was screwed down because of the Alzheimer patients, worn brown recliners lined the wall, and strange smells lingered in the air. Is this how and where we are meant to pass from this modern life? It all seems very artificial and unnatural to me.

The plants begin to wither after the first frost. Now the different shades of brown come and eat away at the green. Some plants are very strong and fight the cold very hard. They are prepared with thick skin and stalks, insulated by strong foliage to weather the cold well into December, just before the consistency of real winter weather sets in. But, some of the weaker plants wither almost immediately as though the breath of cool air is a poison. For the annual plants, this is the end, their life just a mere season. They have completed their cycle, this is their last green. For perennials they will hopefully survive the winter and more seasons to come, this is just their last green of the season.

When it finally happened, during the last few hours of Christmas day, I didn't know what to think or say. But all we thought of was this beautiful portrait of her. We all went to the nursing home to see her peaceful body and our Uncle brought the portrait, so we could all remember her like this. There was a first snow that night and I made the first footprints around the park in the dark.

When I stare into her youthful eyes, I see her Grandma face that I grew up with. I also see my mother's face and then my sister's and my own. All of us women have passed this age forever now. But, she is still here inside of each of us, we are all layered together and connected by our common seed. This is why we cry too, because her death calls to surface our own mortality. We will die one day too and hopefully there will be other women who will still see our face in them too.

Each green that passes feels more comfortable now. This is the natural order of things. It is all so simple-a seed, a season, some green. I used to think in more complicated terms, negotiating my green with different ideas. But someday the last green will come for me too, and then your present will be my past too.

Joe McKenzie

Nothing Good

There were boxes in the apartment.
One box was labeled "nothing good."

-Helen Levitt, photographer, ArtNews, May 2009

after she died, old and without family, we opened windows
long shut and went through her things
with what we felt was appropriate detachment
from the emotions that led to their acquisition, gifts
at holidays and birthdays we imagined as joyous days
full of the moist cake of life, like the days she purchased
her closet of shoes that sat polished and ready
for tomorrow, some still born in their original box
favorites bought as reserves and never unpacked
but she knew they were there waiting just in case
she broke a heel or lost a single shoe, the odd OCD
worry of needing just a left or a right to make a pair
and in the kitchen nearly every box and can expired
before her and we tossed or packed it all away
folded clothes for Goodwill
stacked books and records, trashed a lifetime
of trinkets, memories and assorted junk
until we came to a box taped closed
shoved under the bed and labeled *nothing good* —
and that made us stop our detached destruction
brew a pot in her Mr. Coffee and speculate
about what she might have chosen

to place in the box, to hide under the bed, and
did she do it all at once, going through her photos
or slowly over the years, struggling in weak moments
not to place everything in, or content
that it was just a small box in a long life
and we would all have some not so good stuff
we could never let go of
or it us —
until we finally did.

6 mi W of Cedar Vale

(weather reported by amateur radio)

Around 4:30, a retired farmer reported an observation
from the weather station on his family wheat farm

that a wind of 60 mph had blown a gust of cool air
by his place as he sat alone in his basement

sipping Folgers and monitoring things
which he did most days now he had sold his land

auctioned off his equipment and junk, just
keeping the house he had built with his wife, who

passed this year, leaving behind her sweetness,
the scent of rose from flowers she grew and dried

for potpourri, which he set on his radio to warm each day
rekindling his memory of her and what she would say

about wind, storms and rough times they lived through
out here west of town, where you could see it coming,

but think maybe it would miss you, like it often did,
different than the way he missed her now, feeling her

presence moving him, such a strong gust of her
turning the rooster weather vane of his rusted heart

as he sits drinking coffee by a staticky ham radio
6 mi W of Cedar Vale, Kansas.

Half Crazy

It doesn't matter which half is the crazy side
of a person to an untrained observer
as long as we get to deal with the calm
rational response side when we confront
the beer belly of sanity over a small thing
like a lap dog on a leash,
squatting in the light of an indifferent moon
a sad crescent seeing the dog poop
daily, on the edge of my lawn,
without a scoop in the meaty hand
of the fat guy who holds a red leather leash
clipped to the studded collar of this lame
little fur ball mama's dog, who just wants
relief and is into routine like many of us
so, same lawn day after damn day —
mine, and something about the guy's
t-shirt tells me he drinks Bud,
not light, and he's a proud dog-loving
tax-paying, flag-waving American
who won't understand my half-sane side
as I approach him smiling
with a doggie biscuit and gun.

Grey Johnson

Roads

When I left home
I took this road that stretched
away across the wheat fields
(bye thee bye Dorothy!)
As the bus rolled into sunrise
I thought there's another world
out there down there
at the end of this road
waiting for me

Across the years I've rolled
into many a sunrise and that world
out there down there
is still waiting
I haven't gotten the distance you see
of that road there's always
another and another

My memories are like maps
My days numbered like mile markers

A Windy City Dawn

The “L” car sways and screeches long streaks
of the dawning sun just topping the roofs of Chicago,
Blur of a grainy-bricked building impossibly close...
   And then:
A soft tinkle of breaking glass behind me —
a woman’s quietly startled *Oh!* —
across the aisle, a man drops his newspaper —
stares in wonder at the holes in it
and at the broken window next to him.
  Later, the radio says
someone had been shooting at the “L” that morning:
Those of us in the car —
  didn’t hear the shot that
  barely scratched the woman’s knuckles
  and killed the day’s headlines.

Evening In January

Church bells ringing along the evening street
  sound like your voice a symphony
I turn it's been so long you never answered
  and there is nothing
  only the brittle air
  spider-webbed
  with a memory
  of bells

The Gorgon by Douglas Hoesli

Diane Whato

In the Tropic of Capricorn

Crossing the Sierra Madres,
we hide from tropical murders
of certain ambivalent loves.
Windshield wipers slosh away
great heaps of old, used-up stars
scattering like diamonds on this dirt road.
We call down the shaft of an abandoned
mine, hoping the mouthless bodies
will answer and swallow up our fear.
The glass fogs over from our heavy breathing.
We are here without visa in the city of love.
Here where calves' heads are skinned
and carried in tubs through the market,
where crowds defy gravity and hang
by their toes from the sky. It's too easy
to say we're at peace, but the saguaro
spread their arms over us in blessing.
A small sign divides the good from the evil
but it's possible to cross over in one leap.
A child says good-bye over and over,
And a letter arrives, the one we've been
waiting for, the one we open for news
of what is one the other side of the mountain.

Tet Offensive

He fills small red envelopes
with crisp new dollar bills
for the Vietnamese neighbors
who bring us egg rolls when
they have a party. I think back
decades to the Tet Offensive,
the day of the old war that told.
the generals we weren't prepared.
In my memory, it was a disaster
for our side. He says I'm wrong,
explains in detail what happened.
With Walter Cronkite's avuncular
voice still in my memory, nights
we watched horror unfold as we ate
dinner, I wonder how I got off track
I'm sometimes wrong, but not this
time. Yet, I decide to keep my peace.
Why start more wrong-headed
wars when keeping the peace
seems the better part of valor.

Crossing the Desert in the Summer of Love

If you come to San Francisco, wear flowers
in your hair, we hear on every radio
station between Michigan and Mexico.
We drive the black station wagon, miles
of sand and mountain. I wear my pink
sleeveless dress in the desert heat. Only
whores wear pants in Mexico, you say.
And I believe you. We get to the Sierra
Madres, you are sick from eating fried
turtle steak. I, a Pepsi propped between
my thighs, drive. Clouds below us on
the narrow, sinuous road. I don't dare
look down, but keep my eyes straight
ahead, teeth clenched with hope that
we stay on the road when we are overtaken
by rickety trucks or buses fill with people
who stare, you in the back of the black
car. I drive alone, my dress pulled up.

Boyd Bauman

Spring Eternal

Some people need
more churchin' than others
Dad proselytized
most Sunday mornings
as Mom readied herself
for the Methodist service.
Those rare Sabbaths
his tactic's success
garnered grace for the son
I was off
tin canteen in hand
bivouacking through timber,
pasture and creek
before bursting from the cornfield
to stand at the edge
of our family's spring.

Hallowed be thy name
of my father
and my father's father
for the faith
they mustered
in each seed
and the work of this earth
which brings it to light.

Love thy neighbor
as thyself
as they did
in the dust dry thirties,
filling barrels in the back
of horse-drawn wagons
for farmers to haul
to thirsty cattle and kids.

Upon this rock
I will build my church
for that was where
it was most pure,
I prostrated myself
and drank
in some depth of remembrance
the transubstantiation
of the generations
and it filled me
with as much of the eternal
as I needed to know.

Lava Soap Dirge

Pumice stone.
Cat's tongue.
Salt lick.
Steel file.
#40 sandpaper.
The laborer's loofah.
Rough lover of no foreplay,
you got right down
to the nitty-gritty.

As pall bearers,
distant brethren stand
on Walmart shelves erect
overcompensating —
pledging to warm, moisturize, sooth,
douche, calm, smooth, sexualize
via herb, fragrance, aroma therapy,
pH balance.

You must have dissolved
with the last real cowboy I knew.
The day's dirt smiled
under his fingernails
as he greeted you
with a man's handshake
before an epic battle erupted:

elbow grease vs. combine grease,
volcanic suds unearthing
manure,
alfalfa flecks,
WD-40,
tributaries oozing toward the drain
in molten flow
to lie somewhere dormant

save for those rare occurrences
composite of my muscle memory activates
and my hands are soiled
in honest labor,
then from my core
coagulants threaten to surface and spew
and I would sacrifice all that is pure and good
to be baptized again
in your healing abrade.

Recipe for Making a Delicacy of Spam

Step One: Unseason yourself to a naive
twenty-something.

Step Two: Pour some savings
into a flight to Juneau.
Mix in a ferry ride to Sitka.

Step Three: Increase the employment rolls
of Sitka Sound Seafoods.
Stir in some revulsion
at standing on the slime line
ankle deep in fish intestine.
Add more than a pinch of pain
when promoted to the freezer crew.

Step Four: Garnish every two hours
with a measure of mercy
via a 15-minute break.

Step Five: Scoop plain white rice
onto a paper plate each break
for the first three weeks.

Step Six: Sprinkle some salt on top
the fourth and fifth week.
Simmer.

Step Seven: Splash on some soy sauce.
See how that sets
for a couple more weeks.

Step Eight: Splurge on a container
of the best Spam
your money can buy.
Spread generously.

Voila! A dollop of denial
is man's most savory
of appetizers.

Al Ortolani

Weekenders

We have a small house
on a quiet cove on a busy
lake. Often, when we
step out onto the deck
after days of being absent,
we've seen a Great
Blue Heron, lifting
his wooden body with
ungainly wings into
the grove of trees along
Brush Creek. His nest
is near, fledglings,
a mate for the season.
The lake is artificial,
a frustration for the purist,
the naturalist, dammed
at the confluence of Ozark
rivers. For seventy years
the valley below has
been flooded, the thought
of it, now, murky, eerily
shifts in present tense.
The migration of pelicans,
hummingbirds, geese,
increases sales in binoculars,
water toys, Bud Light.
Weekenders in speed boats
lift cocktails
to the heron's flight, the
otherwise forgotten.

Caught Naked with Her

As a young janitor, working
my way through college, I
stumbled into a painting studio

where a woman I'd known
from the Work/Study Program
posed nude, a black scarf

trailing one thigh. (Easily,
the only memorable moment
in my janitorial career.) Yet,

when our eyes met, I felt
embarrassed for sweeping so well,
for using the dustpan, the little

whisk, for seeing her naked
with a broom in my hand.
In hindsight which is 20/20

I should have excused myself,
backed out with my rubber
trash barrel banging the doorjamb.

Suffering on the Floor of a Fast Food Bathroom Stall I Imagine Amerigo Vespucci in Japan

There's a pattern to my stupidity,
one where I drift along in a pretty
normal day to day routine,
and then for no apparent reason,
I end up on the floor of a toilet stall
in gut-wrenching pain, trying to
negotiate a method to puke
and shit my brains out at the same time.
I know what you're thinking
that I'd gone on a drinking binge
and was now paying for it in a john
without toilet paper (which I didn't
realize until too late). But my illusions,
if you will, aren't facilitated by alcohol.
I'm pretty much free range in grandeur.
I took the Dante's Inferno Challenge
at a sushi bar, for which I was awarded
a white t-shirt, printed up like the
release form I signed, guaranteeing
the owners that I would not sue them
if I ended up like I ended up.
It was a spontaneous moment,
but I was certain I could put to shame
a full ghost pepper sushi roll

in five minutes without recourse
to water, or milk, or beer, or crackers,
or bland white rice, while the sushi chefs
and waitress and manager and a few
customers took photos. I think
what confused me was the mix
of the Italian literary allusion
and the haiku of a little fish
wrapped in seaweed.
I felt like an early Italian explorer
sailing into Yokohama or Osaka,
wooden keel cutting towards paper houses,
and then at anchor, bartering terza rima
for puffer fish. But I was mistaken.
The Portuguese sailed to Japan first,
not the Italians, and certainly,
not Amerigo Vespucci.

The Ticket Booth by Douglas Hoesli

Jackie Magnuson Ash

December's End

Her mother stands over a box of stars and angels
in the west bedroom upstairs, the one
with the attic door. She's putting away
Christmas, face pale, mouth pulled down
like a bulldog, eyes troubled. She's missing
something, a wise man, maybe, or a shepherd.
That's the day everyone first sees it—
melancholia tinged with angst.

Next Christmas family carries on
as if nothing has changed. They gather
at the farm, bring crock pots of soup,
gifts for the tree, bottles of wine.
They never find what she lost—wise man
or shepherd. They still can't say what it was.

Ice Storm

A tree branch breaks in the gloom,
the sound like the crack of a rifle.
It clatters against the barn, glazed
power line caught in its tangle.
She stands frozen, bundled
in coat and scarf, awed by this
fantasy landscape—Lewis' Narnia
where it's always winter.

Her mother's house—the one here
on the farm, this dark icebox—
stings the back of her head.
It's empty. No, not empty.
She's moved her own things in—
they have, her husband and she.
Some boxes wait, unopened.

I feel like I've died—
Her mother said this last spring,
after family urged her to town.
She has her things, writing desk,
brass bed, red chair, but they're
out of place, like her, buried
in white-walled silence.

Snap—another branch.
Ice shatters in little pieces.

When Stars Are More than Stars

They pierce night with glimpses
of glorious dawn, explosions

out of darkness. We witness
icy void set afire forever
and ever. Without stars

earth would be nothing,
we would be nothing.

Here is love—
green sprout
heron skimming the water.

Michael Hathaway

beast

pirate-eyed
July moon cat

funny clown
& star lover

wise secret
nightkeeper

tender chin
kisser

protective
nightwatcher

pillow hogger

perfect
life companion

beyond sunday school

He seems like a scary giant
who can create Life and Death out of boredom,
invent Love when he's lonely,
Hate because he's angry

Then he seems like a primitive child,
playing about with his planets/marbles,
exploding gasses, pretty colors and sounds.

Throughout his playground universe,
space stuff pops, flies, explodes, crashes
to his amused delight.

Light years away from the scope
of any human eye or comprehension,
creation burns, freezes,
creates color & light,
changes,
remains the same.

Huge orbs travel given paths,
minute by minute,
eon by eon,

as little bugs live and die
as we live and die
God plays.

Birthright

My horoscope declares,
Your father will be able to
leave you very little.

When my father remarried and moved across town,
he gave me a little house on two acres,
the house I grew up in,
the safest place on earth,
where Mother's ashes are planted
and the remains of every pet
I ever loved.

Along with an armful of Hank Williams, Sr.
and Connie Smith records,
this came with a lifetime of lessons by example
in integrity, a work ethic beyond reproach,
and an undeniable sense that I was loved
no matter what.

Kyle Laws

Nothing Is As Lonely As God on Horseback in the Desert

All I hear are complaints of saddle sores,
the heat, distance without points
of reference, and the mirages—
those seeming spots of oil on the trail.

I would give anything if those spots
were runoff from cold draft beers
pulled from a silver keg under a bar—
wiped as many times as stars in a desert sky
and still it shines with oil
of the neighbors' hands—
the ones who come to talk after the shift.

That's what I miss—
the men with bravado of a well-worked day,
the women who instead of resenting
the time spent with me
know it clears a way to conscience,
not quite a prayer but a glass raised
to what's just beyond reach
that opens a path,
a way home
to the front door.

Southwest Wink Into Darkness

But there wasn't a sound. Only wind in the trees,
which blew the wires and made the lights go off
and on again as if the house had winked into
the darkness.

—*The Great Gatsby,* F. Scott Fitzgerald

No trees, only wind in late September,
which blew wires from a pole lower
than it should be, not old growth, but
whatever new there was in New Mexico,
down from Farmington, up from Gallup,
not far from Chaco Canyon as the crow
flies, but by road .... I stop listening
to directions after three minutes.

On painted pew, I look down at Navajo
used by code talkers in World War II,
linguistics not my strength. I have
enough trouble with French and Creole,
my Spanish only slightly better after
three high school years when I told
myself I was coming west. Lights flick
off and on in a pattern not Navajo,
but like the shafts of light in a forest
of stunted trees painted by Emily Carr.

When we discussed the exhibit of three
at breakfast after the Santa Fe Opera,
two women at the table thought Emily
held up better than Kahlo or O'Keeffe.
I remember having similar thoughts
as Todd and Barbara waited while
I stood in front of every painting.
Todd, ever a Dillinger chronicler,
asked if I still wrote of Kahlo, and what
I said was something along the lines
of, *Not now that everyone else does,*
I don't write well in a crowd.

Gatsby's house winked, not strobed
into darkness like a lighthouse on a point.
Lights blink in the stone chapel
over words with too many vowels.
It's the grouping, the crowd, that shorts,
wires twisted around each other whiplashed,
that makes O'Keeffe's simplicity look
shallow, but she was going for what she
looked like standing alone, up on a ridge,
staff and dog at her side.

Stop-Time

Now ... in the stop-time of a photograph, their flaws etched ....
—*The Mercury Visions of Louis Daguerre*, Dominic Smith

What a viewer doesn't realize when looking
in pond, glass, or mirror is—when a photograph
is shot, the image frozen, it captures the ache
in shoulder that causes it to droop, the smile
held too long, or the morning's argument over tea,
no chance for repositioning, a response so old
we no longer know we do it. What is captured
is before, and when we look at that instant of time,
we do not recognize ourselves because it is not
who we see.

You can hear Georgia and Stieglitz arguing—
Photography is able to flatter or embarrass
the human's ego by registering the fleeting
expression of a moment. But psychological
records registered in this way have nothing
to do with aesthetic significance as it seems
to be understood today,

she favoring the lasting emotion of elongated
curve and line with pigment, and he the honesty
of the moment, as they lie sprawled, conversing,
in the slow-time after love.

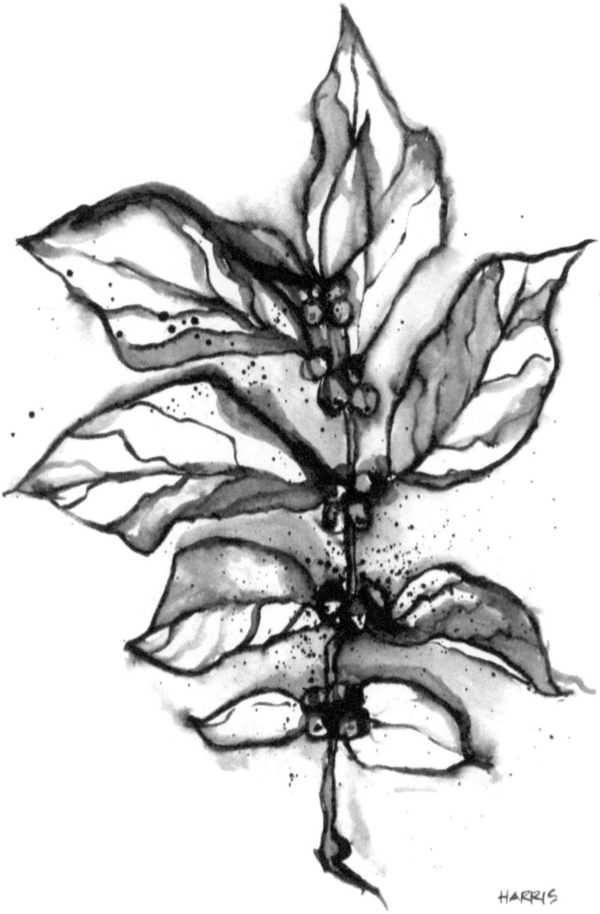

Leaf One by Pamela Harris

Timothy Tarkelly

Family Radio, Spring 1945

The girl laying at her mother's feet.
The radio projecting Ike's voice again,
filling the room like the dusty den at sunset
the beams fuller than they've ever been.
Europe sounds awful, she thinks,
drawing a wild, jagged map of her own,
but finding the Rhine looks just like her own river,
shallow, lazily flowing at the back of town.

How hard could it be to cross? she shrugs
and imagines her own voice filling a den,
commanding attention, other girls shivering
at big, scary army words that glide above,
reflecting a thought she'll never forget,
stuck in the beams, but still shining.

The Cadet Reads of Gaucho Life

To live Zane Grey, to be the man against the elements, but this time in a different continent. The air has to be sweeter, the girls finer. To hear *gringo* and buckle with pride, pretending insults don't stick this far south.
To wear it, singing half-hearted Spanish versions of the *Home on the Range* and whistling at the sunset. To ride through a distant richer prairie, to reach from his horse and feel the tickle of exotic green, rather than the Kansas wheat. To have his *zumo* in the morning, sticky and sweet on the lips, to savor it, to have breakfast fold into the day, not crack like a damn whip. To wake up and make the Earth give under his whim, under iron horse shoes in whatever direction he feels like. To look down and never have to see the brass-buttoned breasts of academy gray again, his boots now polished with the untouchable stink of a real man's work, back to the roots, the earth-tone ponchos protecting *la pistola, el látigo,* protecting him from the pampas winds. To see a sunset, the same old sunset, but from the other side.

Patton

That guy? With the leather leggings in the heat? With the Caesar complex and a laurel hanging from his bunk? With a fevered eye set on every foreign capital? With the hand dropped in anger against a tired soldier, a child – a hand under the weight of an ego so big, yet so fragile? That guy with a permanent spot in Ike's doghouse, on a dirty and fuel-stained blanket? With the cold shoulder to every order, unless he thinks he thought it first? That would-be Odysseus son of a bitch? That perpetual spearhead, free ranging, putting a bunch of men in the middle of shit just to watch himself survive it? With a woman at home, no doubt, just waiting for him to get off his high hero hopes and come on home? With his arms crossed, feet tapping at the Moselle River, thinking he should be the one calling the shots, wearing the stars, talking like a god on the radio? That guy? Pentathlete, but repeated math, leader of men, but can't wash the Welsh out, can't show up to class, can't just look California in the eyes and own it, gotta die in traction? From a car crash in peace time? In peace time?

Rikki Santer

How to Cohabitate with a Kaleidoscope

after *Infinity Mirrors* by Yayoi Kusama
Cleveland Museum of Art; 2018

arthropod eyes for equilibrium polka dots eye you as you eye them in your endless chamber silver balls float among the hosta in this hot house mirror mirrored door claims you shuts you in she promises *in a most animated manner* modest proscenium launches you into the pleats and folds of abyss flickering gold lanterns dangling crystals polymath for your sensory pilgrimage cloth organs swim in the effervescence ain't no peep show but a long long story that refracts your body melts you away into the infinite spread tentacles bedazzle in ambrosia of space-time kabocha squash like paper lanterns guide your ancestors back to you on the gleaming waters of today's dream stars scatter like sugar another glitterbomb and then another another tumble spin fractal patterns you breathe in pulse with moments of
symmetry symmetry

In the Company of Flowers

after Rebecca Louise Law's installation, *Community*
at the Toledo Museum of Art

Submerge me into this linear bouquet
curtains of plants
trickling down from heaven's grid
rack my focus through the rain
of rhythmic notations
vertical riffs of
ancestral petals
tiny gourds on tender
edge of rattle
little swords of wheat
fuzzy-hearted commas
of whispery fronds
all in a marimba of alchemy
to galvanize this womb of a room into pastoral idyll
selfie travelers transform
become selfless
revere pigtails of copper wiring
chimes of gloriosa daisies
blue larkspur
lavender pulse of little lottie
memories of love or loss try me on
nooks and crannies air-born staccato
shadows harmonize with white walls
membranes waltz onto linoleum floor
yawning of dawn in low hum
the dead never so fresh & syncopated.

More Than They Should

after *A Dangerous Woman: The Art of Honore Sharrer*
Exhibit, Columbus Museum of Art; 2017

Sidesaddle on her gander and in voluptuous
nakedness, Mother Goose hovers above
the unrhyming of her rhymes.
Her canvases are trampolines for curveballs—
steady eyes from an army of nude
Ledas defiant against Rubenesque leers
and unhinged from all slithering swans.
Instead, they demand their posed universes
be picture-locked into liberating subversion—
chairs float, domestic pups screw, a slab
of raw meat prays for us all. An alphabet
of random knives, forks, and plates
punctuate the dangers served up in bold
platters of irony and the owls, those owls
that seem to know more than they should.

Steph Castor

October 10th

boots crossed
ankles laced
coffee paints
foggy head, cozy face

nonsensical
remember to be, make sense, foggy feet
when water pounds
coffee drops

twisted head
cocaine chase
backwards tongue
taste time
amphetamine pace
how many weeks
drinking dizzy

your hair
smells like
warm drum beats
city scenes

mouth feels
like cake
hot tea
the Pearl District
burns perfectly

A Structured Exegesis

I come from foreign liberation and weird
holes in my ears with all shades of pride and moderate
temper as I have bathed with the dolphins and never feared
my own death outside of volatile wind and confederate
shotguns to the six worry lines on my forehead, never cured
of the cocaine coffee table at age nine, defined
as powdered sugar that I refused to blanket on that day's obscured
dessert. It was so pure, white, sweet, and refined,
and I can't help but remember the alimony
and what we left behind, for Mother had to scoot
our home into a garage and store knives next to My Little Pony.
We drove through cacti and snow without pause in commute
to Kansas, then Chicago, then back to Kansas for *love*
is more than just a Mother, but a filthy latex glove.

From the Anglican Priest Who Swears Like a Sailor

We live our lives assuming things will happen.
We are the only animal with an extended childhood.
We have lost our body hair.
It's something that follows.

Let's harvest the body.
The liver is the only organ capable of complete regeneration.
(Put a .45 behind his ear, pull the trigger, and send his family the bill for the casing)

Disconnect the kids from the Life Support System.
Medical tourism:
One fetus is better than three.
Zero is better than one.

They are willing to sell their kidneys to Westerners with money.

Prior to the sixties, they killed babies by keeping them in the corner of the hospital.
This is mostly for your edification.

If you don't really understand microbiology, skip this chapter.

Sexual selection has pushed us to where we are now.
What is the difference between herpes and love?
Herpes last forever.

He had a vasectomy.
He reminds me of my grandfather.
He is totally accessible and absolutely hates George W. Bush.

We live our lives assuming things will happen.
Light as well as time appears in packets.
Eighty-five percent of the universe shouldn't be there.
Dark matter.
No one holds a candle to a chimpanzee.

Leaf Two by Pamela Harris

Jared Smith

So Like the Metal Cattle Cars

I don't know what the kill mechanism is
hidden under the football helmets and padding
and in gun cabinets across family rooms,
but the man downstairs went into his den
last night with his dog thinking doggie thoughts
and his wife outside and closed the door
and put a bullet through his head,

and he won't ever have to worry about healthcare
or Medicare Part B or his daughter's education
or whether the country is great again or not,
or how the universe fell away from his wife
who will lie awake in horror the rest of her life
or remember why he bought that damned tube
of metal so like the metal cattle cars he rode.

Beyond the Heavy, Slow Machinery

The sod houses have vanished from these plains.
They have turned into the roads that dot our hills
and have blown away into sunrise that blinds beginnings.
In the north men build their homes of ice, not stone
but the essence of what fills their veins.

Now the majority sterile as hospitals in white gowns, Auntie
Septic fills our nostrils as we hunt for what grows slow.
Trees covered with paint take a long time to grow
and are further removed from us than mud and straw
slapped together with the lime from old bones. Not
human weather chimes but the frames of small sea creatures
left out in the desert sun too long so long ago they are sand.

Shattered desert glass bottles gather atop these walls,
the skeletons of adobe forts holding back time and progress.
People gather like crows and begin to chant shadows.
Wind listens and has little to say of where we came from.
Distance so vast.

Music that obliterates the heavy, slow machinery we knew,
the earth closer to our skin.

This is the American Dream, and What of Joe

Big Joe hauls the groceries in
from the backseat of a beat-up Dodge each week
with never one sick week in his life, but
he sits at a desk six days of seven turning numbers
forty years after Romantic Poetry at Harvard
and teaching Linguistics at Charlotte and UIC
and he remembers the phyla of each green flower
he sees in his memory as he walks the fields
in memory it is getting harder to breathe and
he stops to catch his breath again and again
with each week he is immortal until he dies.

This is the American Dream,
and where are all the professors?
What magic do they breathe into their lungs
where capitalism fills the desert canyons.
Surely it is something potent, powerful,
and invisible as the oxygen that fills our lungs
and the starlight that fills the night lights their pipes.
This is the American Dream, and what of Big Joe
and all his studies, degrees and hours now gone.

Jason Baldinger

The Hymn to Blood Sport

they drive beamers, porsches and hummers
up northumberland to the golf course
they don't stop for working men
doesn't matter the weight they carry
or that it's ninety degrees outside
they see a worker, they speed up

I have twenty boxes of books
to drop at the local library
nothing exciting, but cheap
and saleable. the guy who's
about my age is excited
all the boxes are uniform
they'll fit in storage easily

I bring the last dollyful
he says, *do you think there*
are any part time jobs open?
I laugh, *I am the part time job*

as if keeping your job
is now a blood sport
he answers back, *you're bigger than me*
you can keep the job

I walk to the van. he says
funny isn't it, all there is is
part time work. I laugh
I have four part time jobs
I juggle. he looks at me
do you think we'll make it to seventy?
I answer quickly, *fuck no!*
it's always hard not to swear
I say, *pardon me if that's harsh*
but fuck no. he laughs, says
if I wasn't working, I'd say the same damn thing

March of the Infidels

it's rained hard
torrential, no visibility
for all but nine
of the last sixty miles

off the highway
greeted by an embankment
covered in small flags
looking like
two hundred and fifty
tiny desk sets
two flags, four blades
of grass, forever patriotic

on the stereo
Bud Powell plays
March of the Infidels
staccato intro
before the head
comes in full swing

Bud, you and I
are infidels
all these flags
tokens of some patriotic
religion, some zeitgeist

where it is no longer
patriotic to question
the rule of law

you were beaten
unconscious by Philadelphia
police in 1945
you heard voices
for the rest of his life

I live in a time
where cops still do their best
to kill black men in the streets

I'm waiting on some voice
to bring sanity to
to a country that's teetering

I'm waiting on some voice
that, like your fingers
across the keys of a piano
still celebrates humanity

Kerouac Go Home

I hear the waitress' footfalls
they sound like roses as they echo
across Avenue B, as they echo
across the Avenue of the Americas
they echo at the intersection of Bleeker
& McDougal where Silsbe can't understand
why there's so many people, sure
he's got a few drinks in him
but I never thought I'd see New Yorkers
turn heads at open indictments of procreation
or at least procreation with the intent
to further the fading bulb of humanity

Jay and Ally say they used to write
Kerouac Go Home on the men's room
wall at the White Horse
Dylan Thomas is bleeding out
the blood trail runs to the Chelsea Hotel
then beyond. I slipped on it when I tried to
remember the last time I had a future

I tried to remember the last time
I saw the ocean, there were mustangs
racing on the Garden State Parkway
there were little hands waving on BQE
I swear there was a liberty torch
in the harbor, its head
struggling above the surface

I’ve snagged myself, a driftwood
sculpture, there is so much debris
the gulls have picked through
the soft shelled and horseshoe crabs
the few untouched are boiling
to burst, but the ocean it still
waves under the twin eyes of lighthouses
it never bothered with magic or loss

Huascar Medina

Nuevo 'Merica

Don't call me immigrant
I am the New American
Striving in New America
as a New American
I am not your invader
Not an animal
Nor criminal
I am a just person
just striving
in a New America
In New America I am
A full time student
overtime worker
volunteering in my free time
If I plan enough ahead for free time
If I can even afford the free time
If my free time is approved
I work hard in New America
3rd shift warehouse
2nd shift my house
Always on call
No days off
Freelance for life
4 jobs a week

Blue and white collar
Don't call me immigrant
I am the New American
Surviving in New America
as a New American
I am not your invader
Not an animal
Nor criminal
I am a just person
just surviving
in a New America
This is New America
Student loans for all
High rent
Higher utilities
Low pay
Rising healthcare costs
The cost of living
-deadly
No living wage
Living enraged
Because my cousins are encaged
For wanting to live in
a safer part of
New America

Don't call me immigrant
I am the New American

Living in New America
as a New American
I am not your invader
Not an animal
Nor criminal
I am a just person
just living
in a New America
Strong and proud
able to withstand
the distance I have traveled
the distance from my family
the distance in between us
the distance of our dialects
the distance in our churches
the distance in our homes
the distance between my ancestors
and my grandchildren
the distance from the streets
to the dorm room
the distance from the field
to the corner office suite

Don't call me immigrant
I am the New American
Dreaming of New America
as a New American
I am not your invader

Not an animal
Nor criminal
I am a just person
just dreaming
of a New America
Old America
don't be afraid
we are all America
North America
Central America
and South America
We are all Americas
We all strive in Americas
We all survive in Americas
We all live in Americas
They are all the same America

We all dream of a greater America
I want you to be paid a living wage
Live in affordable housing
Without college debt
or medical debt
or credit card debt
or a national debt
I want no more racism

I am speaking of a New America
I am part of New America
Whether you like it or not
So please join me

Singing Her Blues

for Ellie Smith

Those stage lights are bright
but never as hot
as the 40-watt bulb
 inside that porch light
 outside your home
that spot light
that searchlight
that second sun

-keeping the day longer than it needs to be.

Your front door is
as far from   backstages
as you will   ever get.

So, when you're at a gig
and someone in the audience
insists you,   Sing your heart out!

        We will glance at each other
        smiling with our little secrets.

You're singing it back in baby
  and that's okay.

            It's none of their business anyway.

Waiting room

I wish   I was   a better poet   able to spell   more than just words.   Conjure a place of peace for us.   Write away   Our ills Our hurt   Our fears   Write away   Our losses   Speak   joy & laughter   health & life   love & kindness   into being   with all the magic   we sometimes feel   in a phrase.   This is not that time.   So I offer   words spelled out   pleading for salvation in a silent way   on a single page   You managed to   misplace under bedsheets   on a hospital bed   in an emergency room. Now I wait pacing   back & forth   with strangers   copy & pasting   another night   of hardship   as anonymous   art.

Land by Pamela Harris

The Players:

Jackie Magnuson Ash grew up in Saline County, on a medium-sized farm, surrounded by a family of readers. After a college education, she expected to weave the written word into the fabric of marriage and children. The passing years gave her more than she could have imagined. She's been published in various journals and magazines, including *PlainSpoken: Chosen Lives, Chosen Words, Kansas Voices (2000-2004)* and Caryn Mirriam-Goldberg's *Begin Again,* an anthology of Kansas poets. She currently lives with her husband in Lindsborg.

Jason Baldinger is a poet hailing from Pittsburgh and recently finished a stint as writer in residence at the Osage Arts Community. He is co-director of The Bridge Series reading series. He's the author of several books, the most recent are *This Useless Beauty* (Alien Buddha Press), *The Ugly Side of the Lake* (NightBallet Press) written with John Dorsey and the chaplet *Fumbles Revelations* (Grackle and Crow) which are available now. The collection *Fragments of a Rainy Season* (Six Gallery Press) and the split book with James Benger, *Little Fires Hiding* (Kung Fu Treachery Press) are forthcoming. Recent publications include the *Low Ghost Anthology Unconditional Surrender, The Dope Fiend Daily, Outlaw Poetry, Uppagus, Lilliput Review, Rusty Truck, Dirtbag Review, In Between Hangovers, Your One Phone Call,*
You can hear Jason read poems on recent and forthcoming releases by Theremonster and Sub Pop Recording artist The Gotobeds as well as at jasonbaldinger.bandcamp.com

Boyd Bauman grew up on a small ranch south of the town of Bern, Kansas (population 200). His dad was a storyteller and his mom the family scribe. Grist for the mill included stints as a flight attendant out of New York City, dude ranch worker and ski bum in Colorado, and King Salmon fisherman in Alaska. Boyd has taught English in Hiroshima, Japan and Saigon, Vietnam. He is currently a librarian and writer in the Kansas City area. Boyd lives with his lovely wife Lisa and their little poets Haven and Milly. Visit him at boydbauman.weebly.com.

Roy J. Beckemeyer is a retired engineer and scientific journal editor who lives in Wichita, Kansas. His latest poetry books are *Stage Whispers* (Meadowlark Books, 2018) and *Amanuensis Angel* (Spartan Press, 2018). His first book of poetry, *Music I Once Could Dance To* (Coal City Press, Lawrence, KS, 2014) was selected as a 2015 Kansas Notable Book. He won the Beecher's Magazine Poetry Contest in 2014, and the Kansas Voices Poetry Award in 2016. He recently coedited (with Caryn Mirriam- Goldberg) *Kansas Time+Place: An Anthology of Heartland Poetry* (Little Balkans Press, Pittsburg, KS, 2017).

Photographer, writer, videographer, gardener, and Midwesterner. Glory Benacka is from Nebraska and holds a B.A. in Visual Art from Eckerd College in St. Petersburg, FL. Living on an acreage with her husband, she is a modern homesteading enthusiast with two energetic dogs who take her for walks.

Steph Castor has slept in many beds and is currently focusing on living a life of pure gold. She acts as a freelance content writer, merchandiser, marketer, photographer, doodler, baker, tattoo shop manager, and all around adventurer. Past work can be found in notable music outlets including *Guitar Girl Magazine, Guitar World, Revolver Magazine, Tattoo.com, Outburn Magazine* and many more. Her first full length poetry book, *Bedroom Music*, was published in March 2019 via Stubborn Mule Press.

Michael Cissell was born in Paducah, Kentucky on October 26, 1972. He was a 1991 graduate of St. Mary High School and attended St. Francis de Sales Catholic Church. Michael obtained his Master of Fine Arts degree from Wichita State University. He taught at Wichita State and The Independent School before becoming a fulltime English professor at Butler Community College in El Derado, Kansas where he has taught for the past five years. He passed away in 2018.

Brian Daldorph teaches at the University of Kansas and Douglas County Jail in Lawrence, KS. He edits *Coal City Review*. His most recent book of poems: *Ice Age/Edad de Hielo* (Irrupciones P, 2017).

Harley Elliott lives in Salina Kansas. He is the author of ten books of poetry, including *Darkness at Each Elbow* and *Animals That Stand in Dreams* (Hanging Loose), and *The Monkey of Mulberry Pass* and *Fugitive Histories* (Woodley), as well as a memoir, *Loading the Stone* (Woodley).

Dennis Etzel Jr. lives with Carrie and the boys in Topeka, Kansas where he teaches English at Washburn University. He has an MFA from The University of Kansas, and an MA and Graduate Certificate in Women and Gender Studies from Kansas State University. He has two chapbooks, *The Sum of Two Mothers* (ELJ Publications 2013) and *My Graphic Novel* (Kattywompus Press 2015). His first poetic memoir *My Secret Wars of 1984* (BlazeVOX 2015) was selected by The Kansas City Star as a Best Poetry Book of 2015. *Fast-Food Sonnets* (Coal City Review Press 2016) is a 2017 Kansas Notables Book selected by the State of Kansas Library. In addition to *My Grunge of 1991's* publishing in 2017, *This Removed Utopia* (Spartan Press 2017) was published as part of the Kaw Valley Poetry Series. He is a TALK Scholar for the Kansas Humanities Council and leads poetry workshops in various Kansas spaces. Please feel free to connect with him at dennisetzeljr.com.

Pamela Harris is a graphic designer who also draws and paints. In her personal work, she often feels the urge to loosen up, going beyond the limitations that come with client design work. *There's a certain satisfaction in putting ink or paint on paper and watching what it does on its own, without too much interference from me*, says Pamela. In her design career, Pamela has been employed by print shops, ad agencies, design studios, and by corporate marketing and art departments. She has operated her own design business since 2005, offering print and web design, illustration, and marketing services. More of her work can be seen at PamelaHarrisDesign.com.

Michael Hathaway lives in St. John, Kansas in his childhood home with his family of felines. By day, he works as Keeper of History for Stafford County, and by night edits and publishes *Chiron Review* literary journal which he founded in 1982. He's worked many day jobs to enable his poetry habit including newspaper typesetter/compositor, society editor, librarian, janitor, chauffeur, painter, wallpaperer, ladies clothing store clerk, babysitter, pet-sitter, house-sitter, and living assistant to the mentally disabled. He served 12 years on the Goodman Library city board, and currently serves as secretary/treasurer for the Stafford County Central Democratic Party. In 2008, he accidentally became an ordained minister of Spiritual Science (which has its roots in Theosophy and Gnosticism). He's had 12 books of poetry and prose published, as well as 300+ poems in journals and anthologies. He was founding chairman of Poetry Rendezvous that celebrated its 30th anniversary in 2018. For more information about *Chiron Review*: http://www.chironreview.com.

Thaddeus Haverkamp was raised in Kearney, Nebraska where he received (somehow) his B.A. in English literature. He moved to Lawrence, Kansas in 1995 with the intention of housesitting for one summer. So, mostly through inaction, he has made Northeastern Kansas his permanent home.

Douglas Hoesli: *As a Salina native and wheelchair user a majority of my photographs have been taken around and on our city streets. Being around the arts a majority of my life, I have always felt that has bled into how I compose the world around me. As a photographer I have gotten a lot of inspiration from around and within our downtown Santa Fe Area. Photographically I am interested in the simple spaces, subjects and objects people tend to pass by day to day but rarely notice. Seeing a simplistic beauty of a semi urban landscape wether that be a lonely bike rack or faded out graffiti in the grime of a back alley has always appealed to me. Pushing my chair throughout the streets and alleyways photographing what presents itself to me is where I am most comfortable as a artist.*

Grey Johnson is an unrepentant hippie geezer. Prankster. Dharma Bum. Digger. Etc. This book is *his first serious publication since, well, Nixon was booted.* He lives in Kansas.

Stephen Johnson is a Senior Lecturer in the English Department at the University of Kansas. He has published in *Puerto del Sol, Coal City Review, Physics of Context, Mikrokosmos,* and the *Kansas City Star.* He learned how to cuss from his grandmother, to read from the old timey testaments, and to write from carpenters, mechanics, and fishermen.

Susan Kinney-Riordan has a Master's Degree from Godderd College. She had a book published in 2006, titled *I Wanted A Poem About Kansas.* She has lived in Kansas all her life and has had her poetry published in several journals.

Founding member of White Buffalo and columnist for the Morning Sun, J.T. Knoll is the author of *Paperboy, True Stories, Entry / Exit Point, Chorus Line, Where the Pavement Ends* and *Fetch Crazy*. The collection, *Ghost Sign*, co-authored with Al Ortolani, Adam Jameson, and Melissa Fite Johnson was selected as a Kansas Notable Book for 2017. He lives, with his wife, Linda, and Arlo the Labradorian on Euclid's curve in Pittsburg, Kansas where he is a professor emeritus at Pittsburg State University and operates Knoll Training and Consulting.

Kyle Laws is based out of the Arts Alliance Studios Community in Pueblo, CO where she directs Line / Circle: Women Poets in Performance. Previous collections include *Faces of Fishing Creek* (Middle Creek Publishing), *So Bright to Blind* (Five Oaks Press), and *Wildwood* (Lummox Press). With six nominations for a Pushcart Prize, her poems and essays have appeared in magazines and anthologies in the U.S., U.K., Canada, and France. Granted residencies in poetry from the Massachusetts Museum of Contemporary Art, she is one of eight members of the Boiler House Poets who perform and study at the museum. She is the editor and publisher of Casa de Cinco Hermanas Press.

Gary Lechliter's work has recently appeared in many poetry journals and anthologies. He has published three full-length books of poetry. His newest book *Off the Beaten Path* is published by Woodley Press. Gary is the managing editor of *I-70 Review.*

"Tender but tough." That's how one poet characterized Linda M. Lewis's poems of love and spite, loss and triumph. Linda gratefully accepts the appraisal. A professor emerita of Bethany College in Lindsborg, Kansas, she has been an activist, critic, educator, editor, wife, mother, and grandparent. She is the author of numerous critical essays and four books: *The Promethean Politics of Milton, Blake, and Shelley; Elizabeth Barrett Browning's Spiritual Progress; Germaine de Staël, George Sand,* and the *Victorian Woman Artist*; and *Dickens, His Parables, and His Reader*. This is her first volume of verse.

Melvin Litton has published three novels: *CASPION & the White Buffalo; GEMINGA;* and *I, JOAQUIN* – all from Crossroad Press. His stories and poems have appeared in *Chiron Review, Mobius, Foliate Oak, Floyd County Moonshine, Pif, First Intensity, Broadkill Review, The Literary Hatchet, Bards and Sages,* among others. He has two poetry chapbooks: *From the Bone* (Spartan Press) and *Idylls of Being* (Stubborn Mule Press); plus a short story collection *Son of Eve & other Tales* forthcoming from Stubborn Mule. He is a retired carpenter and lives in Lawrence, KS with his wife Debra and their shepherd Jack. He also writes and performs songs as The Gothic Cowboy and with The Border Band: www.borderband.com

Anne Macker has been doing her art full time for 20 years. She paints on gourds and canvas and is a founding member of the Santa Fe Artist's Market. She lives and works in Santa Fe, New Mexico.

Joel E Matthews is a Nebraska-born farm-boy who le the corn elds for the wheat elds of Kansas. His rst life was as a psychotherapist, where he learned how to put ego aside and walk for miles in shoes not his own. His second, and current, life is as a univer sity instructor where he gets paid to be a nerd about science, culture, and other cool things. You can frequently nd him standing outside talking to birds, bugs, squirrels, and the many rabbits who live in his unkempt backyard. He can also be found in his other natural habitat: the couch; where he reads, writes, watches documentaries, and plays with Lego bricks.

Joe McKenzie grew up in Philadelphia, went to colleges in Pennsylvania, Kansas and Colorado. He enjoyed a long career in libraries, while writing as many poems as would come, retiring as Director of the Salina Public Library. He has been active in the community and continues to volunteer. He has been commissioned to write and read a series of poems on Andy Warhol's electric chair paintings at the Salina Art Center. He was a New Voice Award winner as part of the Annual Spring Poetry Reading Series in Salina, Ks. He lives with his wife, Mary Lou, in Salina, visits his granddaughters in Kansas City often and enjoys traveling to see his son and daughter-in-law in France and his family on the east coast.

Huascar Medina, Poet Laureate of Kansas (2019-2021), is the Lit Editor for *seveneightfive magazine* and a playwright. He's a member of Topeka's Speak Easy Poetry Group and the Red Tail Collective in Lawrence. Recent works published can be found in the *Latino Book Review* (2019), *Flint Hills Review* (Summer 2019), *Finding Zen in Cowtown* (Spartan Press 2018), and *Kansas Time & Place: An Anthology of Heartland Poetry* (Little Balkan Press 2017). His first collection of poems is titled, *How to Hang the Moon* (Spartan Press 2017). His second book of poetry, *Un Mango Grows in Kansas* is forthcoming in 2019.

Caryn Mirriam-Goldberg, Ph.D., the 2009-13 Kansas Poet Laureate is the author of two dozen books, including *Miriam's Well*, a novel; *Everyday Magic: A Field Guide to the Mundane and Miraculous*, and *Following the Curve*, poetry. Her previous work includes *The Divorce Girl*, a novel; *Needle in the Bone*, a non-fiction book on the Holocaust; *The Sky Begins At Your Feet*, a bioregional memoir on cancer and community; and six poetry collections, including the award-winning Chasing Weather with photographer Stephen Locke. Founder of Transformative Language Arts at Goddard College, Mirriam-Goldberg also leads writing workshops widely. www.CarynMirriamGoldberg.com

Al Ortolani's newest collection of poetry, *On the Chicopee Spur*, was released from New York Quarterly Books in 2018. *How Wally Lost His Thumb and the Boy Scouts Became Cannibals*, a mix of old and new "Wally poems" also appeared from Spartan Press the same year. A previous collection, *Ghost Sign*, co-authored with J.T. Knoll, Adam Jameson, and Melissa Fite Johnson was selected as a Kansas Notable Book for 2017. In 2019, Ortolani was a winner of the Rattle Chapbook Series Award. He is the Manuscript Editor for Woodley Press in Topeka, Kansas, and has directed a memoir writing project for Vietnam veterans across Kansas in association with the Library of Congress and Humanities Kansas. After 43 years of teaching English in public schools, he currently lives a life without bells and fire drills in the Kansas City area.

Americana songwriter and Kansas-City-based storyteller K.W. Peery is the author of eight poetry collections: *Tales of a Receding Hairline; Purgatory; Wicked Rhythm; Ozark Howler; Gallatin Gallows; Howler Holler; Bootlegger's Bluff; Cockpit Chronicles.* He is founder and co-editor of *The Angel's Share Literary Magazine* (Shine Runner Press). His work is included in the Vincent Van Gogh Anthology *Resurrection of a Sunflower, The Cosmic Lost and Found: An Anthology of Missouri Poets* (Spartan Press), *Best of Mad Swirl Anthology 2018* and the Walsall Poetry Society Anthology, *Diverse Verse II & III.* Credited as a lyricist and producer, Peery's work appears on more than twenty studio albums over the past decade. Website: www.kwpeery.com

Cal Louise Phoenix was born, raised, and educated in Kansas, where she continues to reside. Her poetry, fiction, and nonfiction have appeared in literary publications since 2010, including her essay "Renovating Shabbat," which won the Beecher's 2015 Contest in nonfiction. Her first book, *Tracing Ghosts*, was published by Spartan Press in the fall of 2018. She is currently pursuing a license in substance abuse counseling.

Kansas Poet Laureate (2017-2019), Kevin Rabas teaches at Emporia State University, where he leads the poetry and playwriting tracks and chairs the Department of English, Modern Languages, and Journalism. He has ten books, including *Lisa's Flying Electric Piano,* a Kansas Notable Book and Nelson Poetry Book Award winner, and *All That Jazz.*

Rikki Santer's poetry has appeared in numerous publications both nationally and internationally including *Ms. Magazine, Poetry East, Margie, The Journal of American Poetry, Hotel Amerika, Crab Orchard Review, Grimm, Slipstream* and *The Main Street Rag.* Her work has received many honors including four Pushcart and three Ohioana book award nominations as well as a fellowship from the National Endowment for the Humanities. Her seventh collection, *In Pearl Broth*, was published this spring by Stubborn Mule Press. She lives in Columbus, Ohio. Please contact her through her website: www.rikkisanter.com

Jared Smith is the author of 14 books of poetry, 2 CDs, and stage productions in New York and Chicago. He has served on the Editorial Boards of *Home Planet News, The New York Quarterly, Turtle Island Quarterly*, and *The Pedestal Magazine,* as well as on the Board of Directors of literary and arts non-profits in New York, Illinois, and Colorado. Jared has taught at New York University, La Guardia Community College, and Illinois Institute of Technology. He has also worked as Vice President of a consulting company, Associate Director of Education and Applied Technology Research at Institute of Gas Technology; Special Advisor to Argonne

National Laboratory; and as a technical advisor to The White House under President Clinton. He lives in Colorado, where he spends much of his time in a rustic log cabin in Roosevelt National Forest.

Timothy Tarkelly's poetry has been featured by *Paragon Journal, Haunted Waters Press, Cauldron Anthology, Peculiars Magazine, GNU Journal, Origami Poems Project,* and many others. He was recently named an Honorable Mention for the Golden Fedora Poetry Prize by *Noir Nation*. When he is not writing, he works as a teacher in Southeast Kansas.

Patricia Traxler, a two-time Bunting Poetry Fellow at Radcliffe, is the author of four poetry collections and a novel, and has edited two anthologies of Kansas memories dating from 1910-1975. Her poetry has appeared widely, including in *The Nation, The Boston Review, Agni, Ploughshares, Ms. Magazine, The LA Times,* and *Best American Poetry*. She has read or served as resident poet at many universities, including Ohio State, Harvard University, Kansas University, the University of Montana, Utah State, and the University of California San Diego. Traxler received the 2019 Kansas Book Award in Poetry for *Naming the Fires.*

Diane Wahto: *When my three sons left for college, I entered the MFA program at Wichita State University. I entered the buzz saw of critique workshops full of hope. However, after a few weeks I planned to drop out of the program, Robert Dana, a visiting professor from Iowa, said I should stay in the program. I eventually learned how to write poetry. Professor Bruce Cutler became my thesis advisor. He entered of my poems to the American Academy of Poet competition. I was awarded first place, with a check to go along with it. After I graduated with the MFA, I taught English Composition at Butler Community College, where I taught for forty plus years. I'm still writing poetry and getting published. I'm also a co-editor for three editions of 365, the anthology of poets who post to the Facebook, "365 Poems in 365 Days." I've published two books of poetry. Leap of Faith, is a self-published book with the help of my son and his MAC computer. My second book, "The Sad Joy of Leaving," was published by Blue Cedar Press. As president of District 5 of the Kansas Authors Club, I've gotten to know poets from around the state. I also belong to four poetry groups, Poets in Hiding, Women Who Write, Thursday Group, and Basement Bards. I owe thanks to everyone in those groups for their close and careful reading of my work. I especially appreciate Roy Beckemeyer, Robert Dean, and Ronda Miller for their support. In May, my poem, "In Answer to W.B Yeats," I received the first place award in the Kansas Voices for the traditional poetry category, as well as winning the best poet award. My husband, our little dog Annie, and I live in Wichita's Old Town in a house that's almost a hundred years old.*

This project was made possible, in part, by generous support from the Osage Arts Community.

Osage Arts Community provides temporary time, space and support for the creation of new artistic works in a retreat format, serving creative people of all kinds — visual artists, composers, poets, fiction and nonfiction writers. Located on a 152-acre farm in an isolated rural mountainside setting in Central Missouri and bordered by ¾ of a mile of the Gasconade River, OAC provides residencies to those working alone, as well as welcoming collaborative teams, offering living space and workspace in a country environment to emerging and mid-career artists. For more information, visit us at www.osageac.org

Osage Arts Community

www.ingramcontent.com/pod-product-compliance
Lightning Source LLC
Chambersburg PA
CBHW030113100526
44591CB00009B/384
* 9 7 8 1 9 5 0 3 8 0 0 5 3 *